Foundation of
Nigerian Traditional Music

Samuel Ekpe Akpabot, Ph.D.
Institute of African Studies
University of Ibadan, Nigeria

Spectrum Books Limited, Ibadan

Spectrum Books Limited
Sunshine House
Second Commercial Road
Oluyole Estate
PMB 5612
Ibadan
Nigeria

In association with Safari Books (Export) Limited
Compendium House
1 Wesley Street
St Helier
Jersey
Channel Islands, UK

© Sam Akpabot

All rights reserved. This book is copyright and so no part of it may be reproduced, stored in a retrieval system or transmitted in any form or by any means, electronic, mechanical, electrostatic, magnetic tape, photocopying, recording or otherwise without the express written permission of the author who is the copyright owner.

First published 1986

Printed in Great Britain

ISBN 978 2265 77 2

ISBN 0 94680-20-6

About the Author

Samuel Ekpe Akpabot studied composition, organ and trumpet at the Royal College of Music in London. He went on to the University of Chicago where he obtained a Master's degree in Musicology and later on to Michigan State University where he obtained a Ph.D. He was a Visiting Scholar in the international programmes of Michigan State University where he taught courses in African music in the music department. He has also taught at the University of Nigeria, Nsukka, the University of Ife and the College of Education Uyo where he was Chairman of the Division of Arts and Head of the music department.

Dr. Akpabot who has composed many orchestral and choral works, is author of *Ibibio Music in Nigeria Culture* (MSU Press, 1975) and currently on the staff of the Institute of African Studies, University of Ibadan.

Dedicated to:

Howard Brown
Tekena Tamuno
James Niblock

without whose concern and encouragement, this book would not have been possible.

Preface

Much of the material for this book has grown out of the author's thesis for the Fellowship of Trinity College of Music, London. Since then, a continuing research into different aspects of Nigerian and African music has resulted in some of the views being expanded, others modified and conclusions made more detailed. African traditional music exists in over 40 countries that make up the present continent of Africa; each country adapting generally accepted practices in the continent to suit its regional characteristics. Some of these general practices include the *Call and response* pattern of vocal music; the *bell rhythm* of the gong; the predominant use of the *pentatonic scale*; the *speech rhythm* growing out of tonal inflections of African words; musical instruments used as *symbols* and the use of *polymetres* and *polyrhythms*.

The aim of this book is to present all these facts as they exist and are practised in Nigeria. In other words, we are discussing here African music in Nigeria — which accounts for why the word 'African' is preferred to 'Nigerian' in some of the chapter headings; especially where the author finds that some Nigerian practices are shared by other countries in Africa. Unlike western music, African music is rather difficult to compartmentalise; thus the reader will find a discussion on vocal music, suddenly bringing in elements of instrumental music to make the points clearer.

The transcription here are examples of Nigerian music; but the conclusions in many cases will be found to apply equally to many other African countries. The words of a song may be different; the artistic decorations on a musical instrument more elaborate; but the general idiom inclines many times towards a common denominator.

One problem in writing a book like this is in the use of terminology. The reader will come across words like organum, counterpoint, iambic rhythm, sprechstimme and gebrauchmusik which may sound out of place in describing African music. The excuse of the author (if indeed any excuse is needed) is that African music should be seen as part of world music and as such should be free to use any terminology prevalent in world musicology. A perfect fifth is a perfect fifth whether in Europe, the Americas or Africa.

It will also be found that certain points are repeated more than once; this is a deliberate act by the author to bring some special points home to the reader. We hope that this book will interest scholars seeking some information for further research, students who want one source where they can get as much information on the subject as possible and ordinary laymen interested in finding out just what Nigerian/African music is all about.

A reading list for further study is included at the end of the book. This has been carefully chosen to fortify the subjects under discussion rather than a potpourri of Nigerian and African music sources which can be found in already published materials. Perhaps more than anything else, it is hoped that the book will fulfil a need, rather than merely serving as an academic exercise. Research was carried out over a period of fifteen years among the Yorubas, Ibos, Ibibios, Ijaws, Hausa/Fulanis, Kanuris, Biroms, Edos, Itsekiri/Urhobos and Tivs.

Institute of African Studies, SAMUEL EKPE AKPABOT
University of Ibadan.

Table of Contents

Chapter	Page
1. The Nature of African Music	1
African Melodies	4
Instrumental Rhythmic Patterns	7
2. Defining African Instrumental Music	9
3. Nigerian Musical Instruments and Their Functions	13
String instruments	13
Xylophones	14
Gongs and wooden drums	14
Rattles	15
Trumpet, Bell and Whistle	15
Flutes and Horns	16
Drums	16
Raft Zither and Thumb Piano	16
4. The Talking Drums of Nigeria	19
Wooden Drum	20
Pot Drum	21
Calabash Drum	22
Hourglass Drum	22
Tom-Tom Drum	23
Xylophone Drum	24
5. Nigerian Drum and Gong Rhythms	26
Drum Rhythms	26
Gong Rhythms	31

6. **The African Orchestra** 33
   All-Drum orchestra 33
   Drums plus other rhythmic instruments 34
   Wind orchestra 35
   String orchestra 36
   All-Xylophone orchestra 37

7. **Anthropology of African Music** 40
   Symbol and Rhythm 41
   Song Texts as Culture indicators 42
   Music in secret societies 43

8. **Random Music in Nigeria** 47

9. **Notation, Terminology and Legends** 51
   Notation 51
   Terminology 54
   Legends and Myths 57

10. **Traditional African Music Elements in Twentieth Century Western Music** 62
    Random Music 63
    Involuntary Harmony and Counterpoint 64
    Polyrhythm and Pontillism 64
    Form and Process 65
    Orchestration 66
    Sprechstimme 66

11. **Musicological Approach to Nigerian Oral Poetry** 69
    The Efik/bibios 70
    Style and Content 71
    Performance and Practices 75

12. **Theories on African Music** 79

13. **Nigerian Music in Societal Change** 86
    Religious Change 86
    Educational Expansion 88

14. **African Music as a Culture Indicator** 91
    Music Sound 92
    Song Texts, Legends and Myths 95
    Musical Instruments 98

15 The Cultural Forms of Nigerian Music — 101
Melodic Patterns — 103
Harmonic Structure — 104
Bell Rhythm — 105
Melodic and Percussive Rhythm — 105
Speech Rhythm — 106
Instrumentation — 107
The Forms of Vocal Music — 109

Chapter 1
The Nature of African Music

One of the chief characteristics of African traditional music is its association with social and ritual ceremonies; but whilst this is generally true, it would be incorrect to say that all African music follows this pattern as there are many aspects of it totally unrelated to any traditional ceremony. It is not unusual to find musicians in an African village gathering together after supper to make music in the moonlight just for the fun of it. The music on such occasions may be background for a wrestling contest, a general sing-song in which everyone present takes part, a solo song of praise or insult or an instrumental jam session. In all these instances, the mood of the moment dictates the type of music and its instrumentation.

African music has also been described as primitive by some writers;[1] primitive in this case not denoting a period of history, but rather the backwardness of that type of music. But is African music really primitive in conception? The description of a piece of music as primitive could be seen as a relative term. A band of African musicians listening to a European orchestra playing a waltz with its insistent triple meter, would tend to term the whole proceeding primitive in relation to their own more complex rhythms. In many books on orchestration in European music, African musical instruments like the rattle, gong and tom-tom drum are described as *exotic*. But these instruments are only exotic relative to their importance in a European orchestra. To the African musician, the gong or rattle is as much an important part of his orchestra as the violin or flute is to his European counterpart. For whereas in European music the gong, rattle or tom-tom drum is used to add spice to the main dish of strings, woodwind and brass, in African music, these instruments are very much part of the main dish.

Three chief characteristics differentiate African music from any other type of music. *Rhythmic and metric complexity*, the use of *improvisation* and *form*. It would be wrong to think of African music as being comprised only of rhythm and melody as a close examination will reveal that there are many musical ideas going on in the inner voices which only a trained ear can detect. African vocal music can be a praise song, a folklore song, a song of insult, a funeral song or a cradle song used by mothers to rock their babies to sleep. There are songs associated with men's, women's and children's groups only, divided according to sex and age and restricted by custom to be performed by specific groups. The classificiation of African musical instruments presents a little problem. Composers like the Hungarian Bartock, the German Schoenberg and the Russian Stravinsky in some of their works did not see the orchestra as being made up of separate divisions of string, woodwind and brass instruments as is the classical pattern of European music; but rather they viewed each instrument on the basis of its individual sonority and capability. This is analogous to African instrumental music where the sonority and capability of each instrument helps in some way to determine how it may be used in an ensemble.

Whereas it is possible in African music to have an orchestra made up entirely of drums, it is rare to find an orchestra consisting entirely of strings, woodwind, xylophone or brass except perhaps among the Chopi musicians of Mosambique who have highly organized orchestras of only xylophones. We do know that a string, woodwind or brass instrument is capable of producing a melody; we also know that African melodies have strongly built-in rhythms; but to sustain an Africna orchestra properly, almost all ensembles make use of percussive rhythms, which means including a drum or two in the orchestra, since the drum occupies a very distinctive place in African music.

Musical instruments of the world have been classified as *idiophones*, like the rattle, *membranophones*, like the drum, *aerophones*, like the flute, *chordophones*, like the guitar and *electrophones*, like modern instruments used to produce electronic music.[2] But whilst this helps to differentiate one set of instruments from another in Western culture, it is not quite adequate in describing African instruments because you have instances of an orchestra combining a drum (membranophone) with a gong (idiophone). Since the drum and gong are both percussive instruments, it would make for better understanding if all African instruments are classified as *string instruments, blowing instruments* and *percussion instruments*. All the string and blowing instruments have definite pitches and the percussive instruments are constructed with high, low or medium tones.

This idea of viewing a percussive instrument as having high, low or medium tone is borrowed from African speech which is inflectionary in character; and African instrumental music borrows much from vocal music which in turn is tied to *speech melody* and *speech rhythm*. Let us look at these connections more closely.

Speech, melody, rhythm and dance are usually inter-related in African music. African music is not notated like European music but passed on by oral tradition; and this inter-relationship makes it possible for a dancer to take his cue from the rhythmic instruments and for a melody to be fashioned out of a sentence.

Most African languages are inflectionary in character producing high, medium and low tones; thus the Yoruba word *Oko* (pronounced or-kor) can mean:

Husband — with the same (medium) inflection on both vowels

Hoe — with the first vowel medium and the second high

Boat — with the first vowel high and the second low.

These words can be represented musically thus:

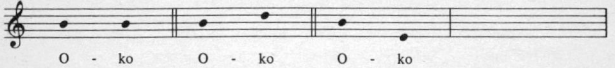

Figure 1.

From the above, we see that the Yoruba sentence: *Agba ti ko kun ahun n'o ni* can be represented musically to form a melody like this:

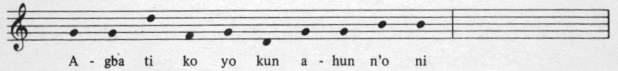

Figure 2.

By repeating the sentence with the correct accent on certain words a tempo in triple time can be established with an accent on the second beat of the bar:

A - gba ti   ko   yo kun   a - hun n'o   ni

Figure 3.

If we wanted to clap rhythmically to that tempo or to play accompanying rhythm on a gong, the accents on the marked words will produce a variation of a rhythm used throughout Africa known as the *bell rhythm* because it is usually associated with the gong:

Figure 4.

From the gong rhythm, a dance sequence can be worked out whose style would depend on the tempo beats and the accent on the words of the song. A traditional dance pattern that makes use of this type of rhythm among the Yorubas is called *Sakara*.

In these examples you will notice two special features of African music. The displaced accent in 3/4 time causing *syncopation* and the use of 3/4 time, 3/8 time and 12/8 time simulataneously producing *polymeter*. The rhythm, melody and dance steps viewed together produce what we call *poly-rhythm* so prevalent in African music.

Sometimes in a moment of absolute gaiety, a musician may improvise with whatever happens to be lying around; an empty bottle, a piece of metal — anything to add to the syncopation of the musical structure. At other times, he may even yodel or shout. This ululation is not as meaningless as an unititiated listener would think; it is a deliberate attempt to enrich the music.

In American black music, you have the same kind of situation, where a member of an ensemble or audience would shout, *go, go, go* or *tell it like it is* during an impassioned performance.

African Melodies

Very many African melodies make use of the *pentatonic* scale, which is a scale of music with five tones as opposed to the seven-note diatonic scale of Western music. But this is not standard practice as we are liable to find music in *tritonic, tetratonic, heptatonic* and *hexatonic* scales. Melodies built around the pentatonic scale are limited in scope. As a rule, African melodies are almost always short, many times fragmentary and very repetitive. They do not modulate to another key and the form can be described as *African Ternary* which means that the first section of the melody is brought back with no modulation in the middle section. Here is an example of an African melody in Figure 5.

The idea of the pentatonic scale is so strong in African music, that even where an instrument, like the human voice or the one-string fiddle, is capable of producing a more flexible melody, a pentatonic melody is still instinctively preferred. But whereas in instrumental music the melody, because of the scale of the instruments, is permanently limited, in vocal music, a clever musician is able to exploit the wider range of his voice as occasion demands. Here is another melody that uses the equivalent of the western diatonic scale at Figure 6.

Figure 5.

You see that unlike the first melody, more notes are used. What of the harmonic context of these melodies? Since the accent is principally on the melody (if in instrumental music) and word (if in vocal music), the harmonic context does not have as much significance as in western diatonic harmony. Generally, the melody is harmonized in parallel fourths or fifths, producing what we call, *strict organum*; it is also sometimes harmonized in thirds or conversely in sixths. Thus, a second voice part to the melody at figure 5 in strict organum would be:

Efik folk tune

Figure 6.

Figure 7.

There is a reason why African melodies are harmonized in strict organum style. Since all African dialects are inflectionary in character, it means that a spoken sentence can have only one fixed curve as in Figure 1. To maintain that curve, a second voice will have to imitate that melody at exact intervals; if it is harmonized in western style to make the second voice part skip about, this will change the contour and meaning of the words of a song. In other words, to maintain the true meaning of the melodic line of a song, the pitch can change, but the melodic curve cannot. This rigid rule is perhaps more true of vocal than instrumental music, where it is possible for a counter-melodic instrument to break this rule and skip about. A common style adopted by African traditional musicians is that of having a fixed moto theme with a virtuoso improvising over this. A typical example of this is when two musicians play on one xylophone as in this example of Hausa musicians from Zaria. An example of strict organum in instrumental music.

Figure 8.

Instrumental Rhythmic Patterns

It is possible to recognize African music purely by listening to its rhythmic patterns.

There are standard rhythmic patterns for many African instruments; this is particularly useful since traditional African music is not notated. If a musician wants to learn how to play a particular instrument like the rattle or gong, he first learns the standard rhythmic pattern of the instrument.

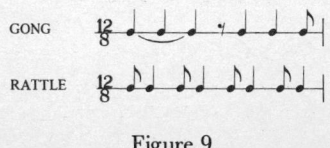

Figure 9.

At Figure 9 we see the standard rhythms of the rattle and the gong. Every African musician who plays any of these instruments knows these rhythmic patterns because they are standard to the instruments. The rhythm of the gong in our example is the one we have already identified, as the *bell rhythm*. Examining those two rhythms again, we discover three rhythmic modes very common in African music: the *iambic, spondee* and *trochaic*. In iambic meter, the rhythm goes short, long; spondee is long, long, while trochaic meter is long, short. If you look again at the African folk tune we examined at Figure 5 you will find examples of two of these rhythms:

Figure 10.

These three rhythmic modes are further examined in chapter 9 under notation.

References

[1] George Herzog, 'Speech Melody and Primitive Music', (*Music Quarterly*, 20, 1934), pp. 452-466.

[2] Curt Sachs, *The History of Musical Instruments*. (New York: W. W. Norton and Company, 1940), pp. 455-467.

Chapter 2
Defining African Instrumental Music

One way to start looking at African instrumental music is perhaps to consider Einstein's evaluation of twentieth century music which he describes an 'orchestral works... in a different way little else (than) shifting the melody from voice to voice — a sort of instrumental monody with rhythmic accompaniment.'[1] This definition of strict twelve-tone style compositions takes in many of the qualities of traditional African instumental music which is linear, repetitious and very rhythmic with a rather sparse use of two or three part harmonies.

Any definition of African instrumental music must take into consideration two chief points: (a) factors which influence the instrumentation and (b) the general characteristics of the various ensembles. The African performer, who is generally also a composer, has an extraordinary feeling for color which he brings to bear upon his instrumentation. The worship of an ancestral god is for him a very serious affair; and therefore, the music for such ceremonies rarely uses any musical instruments that would give an impression of carefreeness. Usually only the drums are used to invoke the spirit of the gods, although there are a few instances where the gong is introduced into the ensemble. It is safe to conclude that the gayer the mood of the music, the more the preponderance of percussive instruments other than drums; the more serious and traditional the music, the more definite and exact the orchestration.

For instance, legend has it that *Obatala*, the Yoruba god of creation had four wives who serenaded him every night singing and clapping their hands in rhythm. The god decided that it would be a good idea to teach them how to reproduce these rhythms on a drum so he had four drums made and named them after his wives — *Iya Nla, Iya Agan, Afere* and *Keke*. These have remained to this day; and in any music for the worship of *Obatala* only these four drums are used.

Any discussion on instrumental music will eventually lead to questions about the tuning patterns of the instruments. The most commonly found scale in African music is the pentatonic scale although Merriam observes that 'while the petatonic is doubtedlessly widely used, the characterization of all African music as pentatonic does not seem valid.'[2] The experience of this author with Nigerian music is that the pentatonic scale is the most dominant scale in the country used by all sections of the community although there are also evidences of the heptatonic and hexatonic scales. There are even cases of melodies using only three or four notes.

Tracy believes that

'... a few African communities may not recognize and employ a single scale or mode only, but may on occasion use more that one scale and from them evolve more than one mode of performance. A naturally pentatonic people may sing not only in pentatonic modes, but several modes.'[3]

The tuning of melodic instruments like the xylophone, seems to be influenced by regional characteristics; and Kubik[4] has written about 'microtonal divergencies which do not seem to occur systematically' in trying to explain why certain notes in a scale do not conform to the recognized pattern. In Nigeria a two-stringed instrument like the lute is tuned a fifth apart, a two-note pot xylophone such as the one used for the Etiliogu dance of the Ibos is tuned a second apart and a two-stop flute is tuned a third apart although there are instances where they are a second apart.

In European music, it is possible to examine the melodic and rhythmic structure of a work, its orchestration, the types of harmonies used and its developmental technique and from these deduce what period of music history it could come from, probably what country and which composer was most likely to write such a work. Under the same premise, it is possible to classify a piece of instrumental music as being 'African' by carefully examining the work under five headings: (a) melodic and rhythmic structure, (b) harmonic context, (c) developmental technique, (d) extemporization technique and (e) instrumentation. The melodic and rhythmic elements are here merged together because to a large extent the melodic structure dictates the style of the rhythmic accompaniment as we saw in the first chapter.

Since most African melodies are built around the pentatonic scale and do not as a rule make use of semitones, their scope is rather limited with a few instances of spinning out the melodies — the second section generally carrying on and bringing to a conclusion the musical idea announced by the first section. By and large these melodies are short, often fragmentary and repetitive.

An instrumental melody many times follows the vocal pattern which is inflectionary in conception; this means that a sentence as previously mentioned, can only have one curve if it is to maintain its meaning. The pitch, however, can differ and the instrumentalist uses most of the technical devices of vocal music and as a result the harmonies in instrumental and vocal music are similar in conception. But whereas vocal melodies cannot skip about, freely virtuoso performers on musical instruments can use any intervals they choose.

There is no developmental technique in African music in the same style as obtains in Western music; rather a whole performance or composition is a *process* growing out of a single germ. In the course of this process, extemporization sets in; and what starts out as a probing melodic or rhythmic fragment announced by a cantor or the leader of an instrumental ensemble on his instrument, is picked up by members of the ensemble who shift this melody or rhythm from one voice-part to another until all the instruments have been heard in one form or another. Next follows a section where the opening motif is repeated many times in varied forms usually by means of embellishments. As this *process* continues, the volume of sound increases and the musicians become excited. There is no modulation; rather, the soloist continues to improvise over a steady rhythmic background until the performance ends fortissimo.

The drum is the foundation of most African music ensembles, fulfilling much the same function as the string section of a classical western symphony orchestra. Drum here is used to include all varieties of the instrument. In Northern Nigeria, the calabash drum (*koria*) is used in every orchestra making use of string instruments. Drum rhythms fit into one of the two main types of instrumental rhythms found in African music — *percussive rhythm* and *melodic rhythm*. Percussive rhythm is that supplied by instruments like the drum, gong, rattle and woodblock; melodic rhythm is supplied by melodic instruments which at the same time maintain their melodic line or fragment.

The nearest thing in European music to an African instrumental melodic rhythm is the *basso ostinato*. But whereas the *basso ostinato* generally controls (or is supposed to control) the harmonic shape of a piece of music, melodic rhythm in African music is a *moto theme* which grinds on regardless of any changes in the overall structure of the music. Thus, the harmonies that occur are incidental results of the contrapuntal movement. It is interesting to note that Bartok's harmonic structure in some of his works especially his string quartets, followed this African pattern. Grout fortifies this view by mentioning that Bartok's harmony 'grows out of the character of the melodies which may be based on pentatonic, whole-tone, modal or irregular scales'.[5] Almost every African instrumental ensemble has a moto theme which can either by a rhythmic or melodic fragment or a combination of both. In an orchestra of percussive instruments or melodic instruments plus percussion, the rhythmic shape of the whole ensemble grows out of this moto theme which acts as a steadying force during a performance.

African instrumental music can be very complex; influenced, as it is, by regional and sociological factors. A researcher into this type of music must be prepared to approach the assignment by placing music sound first and then finding out its sociological and anthropological implications; the approach in many cases has been to fit the music into pre-conceived patterns producing myths and half-truths.

A musicologist versed in the analysis of music of the classic period, will find it impossible to apply the same methods in analysing the music of Schoenberg or Berg; since not only do Berg and Mozart belong to different periods of music history, the thought process and cultural influences that produced the music of these composers is different. The job of the analyst is to find out what those thought-processes are. As with Mozart and Berg, so with African instrumental music. There is nothing 'exotic' about it except perhaps in the fertile mind of the curious.

References

[1] Alfred Einstein, 'The Newer Counterpoint', (*Modern Music,* Vol. 1. November–December, 1928), p. 3.

[2] Alan Merriam, 'African Music', (*Continuity and Change in African Cultures*), p. 72.

[3] Hugh Tracy, 'Towards an Assessment of African Scales', (African Music, Vol. 2, No. 1, 1958), p. 16.

[4] Gerhard Kubik, 'The Structure of Kiganda Xylophone Music', (African Music, Vol. 2, No. 3, 1960), p. 8.

[5] Donald Grout, *A History of Western Music*. (New York: W. W. Norton and Company, 1960), p. 614.

Chapter 3
Nigerian Musical Instruments and Their Functions

Extensive research has been carried out on Nigerian musical instruments of the Ibos,[1] Ibibios,[2] Yorubas,[3] and Hausas;[4] this chapter will, therefore, be devoted to giving an overview of the most prominant of these instruments and their functions and use. As there are over 200 languages in the country, it is possible for an instrument to have as many as ten different names although the functions remain the same in each case. However, some instruments assume greater importance in some parts of the ocuntry than others making it possible for the name of an instrument as used in one region to be widely known throughout the country.

String Instruments
These are mainly found in Northern Nigeria and are widely use by the Hausas, Fulanis and Kanuris, The most commonly found are those with one string (Goge), two strings (Garaya), four strings (Taburu), and nine strings (Molo). The one string fiddle is played with a bow made of horse hair and the soloist produces pentatonic melodies with a range of about an octave and a half. The *Garaya* is of the lute variety with its two open strings tuned a fifth apart. It is plucked with the fingers producing not a melody, but a melodic rhythm used as an ostinato over which the player sings. Functionally, it is played as an instrument for 'going into fits'. This means that a listener, usually a woman, requests a tune on the instrument and dances so wildly to the music that she collapses on to the ground in a faint and is carried away to be revived.

Molo, a nine string harp is also tuned to the notes of the pentatonic scale the nine notes scanning an interval of a twelfth. The sound is very low and in places very faint; and like the *Garaya*, the player sings over a melodic fragment. Incidentally, the name *Molo* is widely used among the Hausas to denote any instrument of the harp variety.

Xylophones

Nigeria is rich with a wide variety of xylophones which can have anything from two to fifteen tuned slabs. The *Gedegwu* xylophone of the Ibos has only two slabs tuned a major second apart; it is constructed by placing the two tuned slabs over a pitcher. There are also the four-note xylophones of the Ibos known as *Ekwe Omaba*; the eight-note xylophone of the Ibibios called *Ikon Eto* and the fiteen-note xylophone of the Hausa/Fulanis called *kundun*. The *Ekwe Omaba* and *Ikon Eta* xylophones used in dance orchestras are tuned to the pentatonic and heptatonic scales respectively. Xylophones in the southern part of the country (apart from the pot xylophones) are usually tuned slabs of wood placed over two banana stems. Xylophones in the Northern part of the country are usually supported by gourd resonators and the player hangs the instrument around his neck during a performance.

It is possible to have two people playing on one xylophone as we saw in chapter one; and when this happens, one player plays an ostinato in parallel fifths or fourths in the bottom register of the instrument, while the other and more skilful of the two improvises over this. But not all xylophones in the ocuntry are tuned to a recognisable scale. Sometimes, as in the *Abigolo* xylophone of the Ibos and a specially constructed four-note xylophone of the Ibibios, the function of the instrument is to imitate phrases and proverbs common to the area; and so the notes (tones) are tuned to reproduce these phrases and not to any particular scale. We can say that any time one comes across a xylophone from the south of the country that does not fall into any of the recognised scales (pentatonic, hexatonic or heptatonic), then the instrument is used to communicate with the community.

Gongs and Wooden Drums

There are two varieties of gongs — the large conical-shaped one producing just one tone and the twin-gong producing two tones which is smaller in size. The wooden drum also comes in small and large sizes and like the twin-gong, produces two tones tuned to a major second, a perfect fifth or a minor second. Whereas the gong is used throughout Nigeria, the wooden drum is prominent only in the south-eastern part of the country among the Ibos, Ibibios and Ijaws. The Ibos call the twin gong *Ogene* and the large gong *Alo*. In other parts of the country the instrument is known by just one name e.g. *Nkwong* (Ibibios) and *Agogo* (Yorubas). Both the gong and the wooden drum can either be played as solo instruments in ritual ceremonies, or in orchestral ensembles where they perform rhythmic and colouristic functions.

Rattles

Six types of rattles are easily identifiable in Nigeria. *Sekere* or *Agbe* rattle is constructed from a dried out gourd covered with netting to which little beads have been attached. It is used almost exclusively by the Yorubas although the Ibos also use the name *Agbe* for a similarly constructed rattle. *Ekput* and *Ekpat Obon* are two ritual rattles used extensively by the Ibibios. *Ekput* is hourglass-shaped with two little pieces of wood tagged on to produce a rattling effect when the instrument, usually made of wood, is shaken. The Yorubas have a similar instrument, which like the Ibibio one, is used for ritual worship. *Ekpat Obon* is a small bag filled with stones which rattle when shaken. The Ibos also use this principle except that the stones are collected in a small woven basket which they call *Ishaka*. These are all examples of shaken idiophones. But there are also scraped idiophones found among the Yorubas (Sokoro) and Huasa (Shantu) which are played exclusively by women. Leg rattles are used by dancers all over the country to add rhythmic colour to their dance movements. Onomatopoeia plays an interesting part in the names given to many Nigerian musical instruments.

For example because of the 'sh' sound which the rattle produces, we have names like *Sekere* (pronounced shekere) and *Ishaka*. The 'ong' sound of the gong has caused the Ibibios to call their instrument *Nkwong*. The Yorubas call the same instrument *Agogo* which is derived from the sound the instrument makes when struck.

Trumpet, Bell and Whistle

The only type of trumpet found in Nigeria is an elongated one without any valves called *Kakaki* used at the palaces of Emire in Northern Nigeria to alert the community of the arrival or exit of the Emir from his domain. The Yorubas have borrowed this instrument which they also use to announce the presence of their Obas or Chiefs, still retaining the Hausa name *Kakaki*. The Bell and Whistle, exclusively used by people in South Eastern Nigeria — Ibos, Ijaws, Ibibios — are two instruments whose origins are hard to trace; although it is probable that they came into the ocuntry through trade by barter that took place in the sixteenth century between the Portuguese and people of the riverine areas like Calabar and Port Harcourt. Only the Ibibios use the Bell (Nkanika) which is like a western church bell in the ritual music of their *Obon* and *Ekpe* societies. The Whistle, shaped like a Boy Scout whistle, is used by the Ibos, Ibibios and Ijaws to indicate rhythmic changes in a ladies dance formation. The whistle is blow by the leader of the dance group to warn dancers of a change in pattern.

Flutes and Horns

Flutes are either end-blown (vertical) or side-blown (transverse). They are made from wood, bamboo and brass with anything from three to five stops. Horns are made from dried-out gourds, elephant tusks, horns of deer and teeth of large wild animals. They are all side-blown as opposed to flutes which are end-blown and are capable of producing up to five tones. The sound and functions of a flute are very distinct from those of the horn in Nigerian music.

Flutes with five stops are usually found among the Hausa/Fulanis (Algaita) and Yorubas (Lara). Three stop flutes on the other hand are found among the Ibos (Oja) and Tive (Amada); and with one or two exceptions, are used chiefly to accompany dancing. Elephant tusk horns are only played by royalty; and the *Uta* gourd horn of the Ibibios occupies a distinct place in Nigerian music because it is the only instrumental ensemble capable of producing four-part harmony when played in groups of four.

Horns are called *Opu* by the Ibos, *Eyin Erin* by the Yorubas and *Oduk* by the Ibibios. The Edos call their brass flutes *Ikpeziken*. The *Algaita* has been described here as a flute although it is an instrument with a double reed. It has been suggested in chapter 15 that perhaps the best way to describe it would be to call it a reed-flute.

Drums

These are discussed fully in the next chapter; but we might add that very large skin drums are used symbolically when played solo, as in the case of the *Tambari* drum of the Fulanis which is struck twelve times when a new Emir of Katsina is crowned; or used in pairs and fours for ritual music by various ethnic groups in the country. Examples of ritual drums are *Igbin* (Yoruba); *Nsing Obon* (Ibibio); *Yogume* (Itsekiri) and *Igba* (Ibo). *Igbin* drum is played for the worship of the god Obatala and *Nsing Obon* is used for ritual ceremonies of the *Obon* secret society. The *Emoba* drum of the Edos is used exclusively at the palaces of the Oba of Benin; and the Ibibios have a unique three-legged drum called *Ibid Ekpo* used for ritual music of the Ekpo society.

Raft Ziter and Thumb Piano

These two instruments are both played by the thumbs of both hands. The thumb piano known commonly throughout Africa as *mbira* or *sanza*, but in Nigeria as *Ubo Aka* (Ibo); *Agidigbo* (Yoruba) is made by hollowing out a circular gourd and placing thin strips of metal over it tuned to the heptatonic scale. The raft zither known as *Ryomka* by the Biroms, is so called because of its shape. It is made of tuned strips of bamboo arranged in groups of three across a flat piece of rectangular bamboo base about ten inches long and four inches wide. Each group of three strips tuned to the same tone and together, the five tones produce the pentatonic scale. Both the thumb piano and the raft zither are played by one man telling story over an ostinato background.

General Observation

This discussion does not exhaust the full list of Nigerian musical instruments as that subject alone could be the basis for a book of its own. What we have done here is to try and select some of the most frequently used instruments and discuss them as representatives of the genre. For example, the bull roarer is an aerophone which operates in a way different from all other aerophones we may come across in the country; and like in other parts of Africa where it is found, it is used in Nigeria for purely ritual purposes as an instrument of social control. When people hear the sound of the bull roarer, they know that members of the Yoruba *Oro* cult are about to make their appearance and lock themselves indoors.

For a comprehensive study of Nigerian musical instruments, the reader is referred to the appendix at the end of the book. Merriam's[5] distinction between function and use in African music is very well illustrated by the horn which *functions* as a symbol of power among royalty and is *used* orchestrally for dance music. In western music, we speak of virtuosos; these players also exist in Nigerian and African music and it is notable that no two drum improvisations are ever the same.

In all the instruments discussed, pitch is not regulated; yet the instrument makers have a definite set of rules for tuning their instruments. Anywhere you go in Nigeria you will find that a twin gong or wooden drum is always tuned to a major second, a perfect fifth or a minor third depending on what part of the country the instrument comes from and for what purposes it is meant. The author has not come across these instruments being tuned to any other intervals.

References

[1] William Wilberforce Chukudinka Echezona, *Ibo Musical Instruments in Ibo Culture.* (Unpublished Ph.D. dissertation, Michigan State University, 1963).

[2] Samuel Ekpe Akpabot, *Functional Music of the Ibibio People of Nigeria.* (Ph.D. dissertation, Michigan State University, 1975.)

[3] Darius L. Thieme, *A Descriptive Catalogue of Yoruba Musical Instruments*. (Unpublished Ph.D dissertation, Catholic University of America, 1969).

[4] D. W. Ames, 'Hausa Drums of Zaira' (*Ibadan*, No. 21 October, 1965), pp. 62–80.

[5] See Alan P. Merriam, *The Anthropology of Music* (Northwest University Press, 1964), pp. 209–227.

Chapter 4
The Talking Drums of Nigeria

All the drums found in Nigeria can be broadly grouped under five headings: (1) wooden drum, (2) pot drum, (3) calabash drum, (4) hourglass drum and (5) tom-tom drum.[1] Between them, these drum categories span all the ethnic groups in the country. The wooden drum is found only in the Eastern States of the country chiefly among the Ibibios, Ijaws and Ibos. The Ibibios call it *obodom* and the Ibos *ekwe*.[2] The distribution of the pot drum follows the exact pattern of the wooden drum. The calabash (gourd) drum known as *koria* is only used by the Hausa/Fulanis of the northern part of Nigeria where it has specific functions. The hourglass drum (*gangan*) is the chief musical instrument of the Yorubas although varieties of it can be found among the Hausa/Fulanis. The tom-tom drum which can either be large of small, is distributed among the Binis, Itsekiris and Urhobos of midwestern Nigeria; and perhaps more extensively among the Ibibios, Ijaws and Ibos of the Eastern states. It does not exist at all in the Northern States; but the Yorubas have large and small varieties of the drum which they use for ritual worship in all-drum ensembles.

The term 'talking drum' as used through the years by western musicologists and observers, is very misleading indeed. This term to an average European unused to African traditions, conjures in his mind a false picture of Africans with bulging muscles banging away at huge drums which are supposed to send messages across bush country.

This is not strictly correct. It is true that some African talking drums were used for this purpose; but it is equally true that there are many talking drums that have entirely different functions. The fact is, that all African drums talk — some more eloquently than others depending on their size, shape and construction. The chief difference between African and European instruments lies in their function and use.[3] Take the trumpet for an instance. The European trumpet with valves can be played by men or women and is used chiefly as an orchestral instrument for large or small groups. The valveless trumpet called *kakaki* in Nigeria is played only by men and has a specific function: heralding the approach or departure of an Emir to or from his palace; for this purpose they use only the first and second harmonics of the instrument and on hearing this played, the community can tell that their chief is either entering or leaving his palace. The European trumpet on the other hand can be played in groups of three or more to produce *absolute* music as opposed to *functional* music. The use of the trumpet is different in European and African situations. But perhaps a closer look at the make, characteristics and functions of Nigerian drums will make this discussion more enlightening.

Wooden Drum
The Nigerian wooden drum (known sometimes as slit drum) is in Sach's classification an *idiophone*[4] with the functions of a membranophone. It is carved out of a piece from a tree trunk with various sizes producing two tones which are always a major second, a minor third or a perfect fifth apart. It can be used either singularly or in groups of two or three orchestrally. When used singularly, it sends out messages from the palace of the chief in a series of rhythmic figures only intelligible to residents in a particular community. These rhythmic figures have been compared to the European Morse code, which they are not. They adhere as much as possible to the rise and fall of speech melody in a musical language which comes easily to the cognoscenti. But perhaps the wooden drum finds its greatest expression in the music of the Ibibio people of the South Eastern State of the country, where it figures prominently in ritualistic and dance orchestras playing a backbeat rhythm special to the people of that area; the figures (1) and (2) refer to the tones of two wooden drums played together.

Figure 1.

To things are happening in this transcription. First there is the rhythm which could have been notated like this:

Figure 2.

But then that would not be complete because it would not be taking into cognisance the melodic rhythm created by playing two wooden drums each with two different intervals: One a major second and the other a perfect fifth — which is why I have notated the rhythm using five lines instead of one. Ethnomusicologists in the past have tried to accurately notate xylophone and flute music of Africa but have tended to neglect the tones of the drums which are selected with care by the musicians and which supply the inner voices in the ensemble in which they are used. Where the tones are as clear as in the wooden drum or the twin-gong, there is no difficulty with the notation; but in other instances where the tones are muffled, the relative pitches of the drum tones should be indicated and an appropriate sign placed under each tone produced indicating that the pitches are not clearly defined.

Pot Drum

The *Pot Drum* or *Pitcher Drum* as it sometimes called is, as its name implies, a large or small pitcher with a hole on the side. Music is produced by the player striking the open end of the pot with the palm of one hand and the hole on the side with the other hand producing two tones which are rhythmical but muffled: the right hand strikes the large opening of the drum and the left hand the small opening on the side.

Pot Drum Rhythms

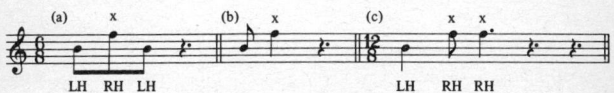

Figure 3.

The sign **x** placed over the note produced by the hole on the side of the drum shows that it is indicative of the relative pitch but not tone. Sometimes the side hole is struck with a flat instrument woven out of rafia instead of the palm of the hand, to produce a more satisfying sound. This drum is an instrument used primarily by women in the Eastern States of Nigeria in groups of two, three or more as accompaniment to their singing. The Ibos call this instrument *Udu* and the Ibibios *Abang*.

Calabash Drum

The word *calabash* is used in Nigeria to mean gourd. The calabash drum is a semi-circular gourd played with two sticks with the open end face downwards. It has only one rather dry tone and is used exclusively by the Hausa/Fulanis of Northern Nigeria to accompany the music of the one-string fiddle called *goge*. An extract from this transcription of a one-string fiddle accompanied by a *koria* (calabash) drum shows how the drummer picks up and highlights the rhythm in the melody produced by the fiddle. Generally, the accompanist does not know what melody the fiddler will play and picks out his rhythm after listening for a few bars — unless, of course, it is a tune that he has heard before.

Figure 4.

It is sometimes possible to have as many as six fiddles playing together accompanied by about two *koria* drums.

Hourglass Drum

This drum is almost a preserve of the Yorubas of Western Nigeria; almost — but not quite because the Hausas of the North also use variants of the drum. As its name implies, it is shaped like an hourglass. It is covered with animal skin at both ends held firmly in place with leather strings, unlike other skin drums that are tuned with pegs. A series of leather strings running from one end of the drum to the other connects the two drum heads. In performance, the instrument is slung on one shoulder and supported under the arm. Graduations of tone are produced by hitting one end with a small curved stick and tightening and releasing the leather strings connecting the two drum heads. It can safely be said that the hourglass drum is the most eloquent of all Nigerian drums. It has a range of an octave and can produce all quarter tones and semi-tones are never used by the players as these do not occur in the Yoruba language which the drum imitates.

The two most commonly used types of hourglass drum ensembles are the *Bata* orchestra and the *Dundun* orchestra.[5] Between them, these two groups represent a fair cross section of the different types, sizes and makes of the hourglass drum variety. The most eloquent of all the drum orchestras is the *Dundun* group which is most frequently used for festive occasions. The *Bata* orchestra is used for ritual worship; and the solo instrument of all these groups is known under the collective name of *Iya Ily* (mother drum).

In any discussion on the Yoruba talking drum, you will always come across the *Godugudu* (two-tone drum); *Kanango* (high pitched drum); *Kudi* (dull sounding drum); *Keri-keri* (low-pitched drum); *Isaju* (medium-pitched drum). These drums are shaped differently but exist under the umbrella of the hourglass drum group. In their tone production, they represent the high medium and low tones of Yoruba speech which they are tuned to represent. Like the wooden drum, which can relay a message when played as a solo instrument, the hourglass drum is extensively used in the courts of Yoruba chiefs to announce a visitor to the royal household or warn the populace of any impending royal occasion or danger to the community.

Tom-Tom Drum

Like the hourglass drum, the *tom-tom* drum comes in different shapes, sizes and makes. This drum is carved out of wood and covered on one end by a membrane although there are varieties covered on both ends to produce two tones when struck on either side. A master drummer, can produce many graded tones on this drum by striking it with a stick and using his curved palm to vary the tones. Found all over Nigeria in one form or the other, it is extensively used in the Eastern and Mid-Western States of the country. The name tom-tom which was given to this variety of drum by western scholars probably derives from its onomatopoeic sound when the very heavy drums are struck. These heavy drums are used almost exclusively for ritual worship and can be played either singly or in groups or from two to seven like the *Igbin* drums of the Yorubas or the *Emoba* drums of the Binis played by six people at the Oba's palace.

Among the Ibibios there exists a rare drum with three legs called *Nsing Obon* which is used for *Obon* masquerade music and only played when a prominent member of the secret society dies. The three legs on which the huge drum stands are symbolic of an unusual person, since the ordinary man has only two legs.

All these drums are tuned by little pegs attached to the side of the drum heads; and the animal skin used as membrane, is specially prepared by the drum makers to make sure that they don't extent or contract upon frequent use. In all-drum ensembles, the largest and lowest sounding drum is the one that talks most eloquently and acts as the soloist. The rhythmic figures played by the other drums in any given ensemble depend on their sizes — the smaller the drum, the less involved its rhythmic pattern. Two types of *tom-tom* drums frequently encountered are two-tone drums, moderate in size and played, hung round the musician's neck and played with a stick in one hand and an open palm, on both ends of the drum which are covered. This practice is very common among the Hausa/Fulanis and the Yorubas. The other type of drum is a long thin one covered only on one end; the musician sits astride on it and drums away. We find this style of drumming in the Eastern States of the country and also among the Itsekiris/Urhobos. Sometimes two small drums covered only on one end are tied together to produce a two-tone effect.

Tom-tom drums are also widely used for dance orchestras like the *Yogume* and *Otogume* drums of the Itsekiris; at other times, these drums are used in concert with wooden drums. When this happens, the *tom-tom* drums are almost always of the small variety so as not to obscure the tones of the wooden drum which in ensembles like this, acts as the soloist, as frequently happens in the *Oreyi* orchestral ensemble of the Ibos.

Xylophone Drum

This discussion will not be complete without a brief reference to a type of melodic instrument found among the Ibibios called *Ikon Ikpa* meaning skin xylophone as opposed to the Ikon Eto, wood xylophone commonly found in the area. It consists of five small drums tuned to the pentatonic scale and played in the same way as a wood xylophone — perhaps the most compelling example of a talking drum. Tuned drums like these are also found in other parts of Africa where they are sometimes given the name drum chimes, which, in the opinion of the author does not correctly reflect the sound produced by the instrument. We could hardly call any kind of membranophone a chime.

What then do we correctly call it, a drum xylophone or xylophone drum? We have discussed the question of terminology in African music in chapter 9; and this instrument falls into the category of instruments with two faces.

References

[1] The word *Tom Tom*, although invented by colonialists, is used deliberately here because its onomatopoaiec sound aptly describes the booming effect of very large African drums. For our purposes in this book, it is used to describe all skin drums other than the hourglass drum.

[2] The author discovered a wooden drum at the palace of the Alafin of Oyo inhabited by the Yorubas who never use this drum. How it got there has not been satisfactorily explained so far.

[3] Alan Merriam in his *Anthropology of Music* (Northwestern Press, 1964) makes a clear distinction between function and use in music.

[4] Curt Sachs, *The History of Musical Instruments* (N.Y., W. W. Norton and Company, 1940) pp. 455-467.

[5] Other drum groups are *Igbin, Akpente, Ikpess, Kete* and *Koso*.

Chapter 5
Nigerian Drum and Gong Rhythms

In almost every transcription of African orchestral music, the rhythms of the drum and gong will be found to be most vital to the overall pattern of a performance. The rhythms of all other instruments in an ensemble will, on closer examination, be found to be either founded on the rhythms of these two intruments, or adapted from them. The gongs come in two shapes: twin-gong and single-gong; and the drums come in different sizes and shapes depending on which part of Africa it is constructed. They can, however be grouped into primary and secondary drums. The primary drums are usually large and the secondary drums smaller in size.

The changes which a master-drummer or a gong player can ring from his instrument are many and varied; but there are certain rhythm patterns that recur again and again and tend to provide *standard rhythms* for particular instruments. If we agree that African melodies are primarily built around the pentatonic, hexatonic and heptatonic scales and that many of these melodies are derived from the tonal inflections of African speech producing in turn *speech rhythm* and *speech melody*, then it is possible to arrive at some basic rhythms which can be found in every African country using these scales.

Drum Rhythms
All drum rhythms in Nigeria can be divided into two; (a) rhythms that exist within an all-drum ensemble and (b) rhythms that accompany melodies and melodic fragments, from a varied instrumental ensemble. The bigger a drum is, the more it is able to *talk* and therefore the more involved its rhythmic patterns. These rhythmic patterns become less involved as we come to the smallest drum which is content to just stress the number of beats in a time signature (tactus).

This is the basic procedure; in actual practice, this may be varied and we can have a small drum tapping out the first two beats of every bar and omitting the third in a piece of music, say in 3/8 time; but at no time is anything too involved attempted. There is also a sociological twist to the organisation of a standard drum orchestra and therefore the rhythmic pattern allocated to each drummer. The author's experience in Nigerian orchestral music, is that four drums constitute an average drum orchestra representing father, mother, brother and sister; where a fifth drum is added it is usually to add color to the inner voice-parts. The most talkative of the group is the *mother drum* with very good reason — a woman (especially when she is excited), can out-talk any man. Two examples will perhaps make this point clearer.

Among the Yorubas, the *Bata* group of drums used in the worship of the god *Sango*, the god of thunder consists of *Iya Ilu Bata* (mother drum), *Emele Ako* (male drum), *Emele Abo* (female drum) and *Kudi* (child drum). The pitch of the voices of the members of a family range from low to high; so the drums in an ensemble are chosen to represent high, low and medium pitches. Thus *Iya Ilu Bata* has a low pitch, *Kudi* has a very high pitch and *Emele Ako* and *Emele Abo* are pitched in between. As in many aspects of African music, there are exceptions to the general rule as in the *Oreyi* orchestra of the Ibos. Here the orchestra consists of four large skin drums and one wooden drum brought in to contrast with the other drums and act as the soloist of the group. Here are three large drum rhythms from Nigeria:

Large Drums

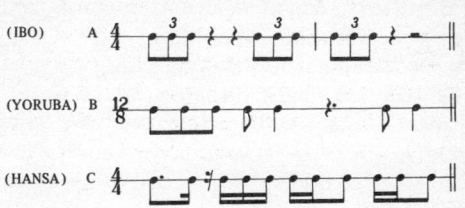

Figure 1.

If we compare these with three small drum rhythms the differences are at once obvious:

Small Drums

Figure 2.

The small drum rhythms at A and B divide easily into two equal groups: the figuration in the first half of a measure being the same as in the second half. At C, with a clear iambic rhythm, the figuration is even easier. At D, there is a syncopated rhythm very common in African drumming.

The large drum rhythms are a bit more complicated. At Figure 1A, the figuration stretches into the first beat of the second measure and it takes a master drummer to maintain this rhythm without getting it all mixed up. At Figure 1B the rest in the third beat of the measure will present some difficulty to anyone trying to maintain this rhythm in an ensemble. The same goes for Figure 1C where the rhythm starts with a skip in the first beat, introduces a rest in the second and sixteenth and eighth notes in the third. Playing this kind of rhythm calls for great concentration and expertise because once the ensemble gets going, a mistake in any one rhythmic part can upset the whole group. Clearly then, it is possible to listen to all-drum ensemble and pick out the rhythms of the large drums as distinct from those of the smaller drums purely by the figuration.

In chapter 4, mention was made of the clabash drum, the pot drum and the hourglass drum which are in many ways unique to Nigeria. The calabash drum known as *koria* is used in Northern Nigeria to accompany a one-string fiddle. Its standard rhythm is of some interest.

Figure 3.

This drum is a small drum but its rhythm is as complicated as that of the large drum stretching sometimes to two measures (as in Figure 1A) instead of one. Another look will reveal that it is also a variant of the bell rhythm used by the gong throughout Africa. The pot drum rhythm most commonly used in the Eastern States of Nigeria is:

Figure 4.

If we play the large skin rhythms at Figure 1B alongside the calabash drum rhythm at Figure 3 and the pot drum rhythm at Figure 4, we have this combination:

Figure 5.

Deciding whether an African rhythm instrumental rhythm is in 4/4 time or 12/8 time is sometimes rather difficult because of the pulse beat common to both meters; but generally the 12/8 meter tends to be slower than the 4/4 meter in actual performance. For an example take these two transcriptions:

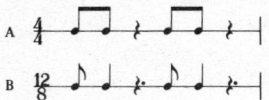

Figure 6.

The difference between these two sounds in actual performance is the difference between what is actually heard and what a transcriber *thinks* he hears. As an African, the author hears figure 6B clearly with accented eight note at the start of the bar; but many non-Africans will most probably *hear* figures 6A and 6B as sounding the same, once again spotlighting one of the problems of transcribing African musical rhythms. If this rhythm was to be used for dancing, the reaction of the dancers to figure 6A would be markedly different to that of figure 6B. A small point it seems, but very important indeed.

In Nigeria, the hourglass drum or Yoruba talking drum as it is sometimes generally referred to, is played in groups of four or five when used for dance music; and in between each spontaneous outburst of improvisation by the soloist/leader of the group, a recurring rhythmic pattern can be detected:

Figure 7.

This pattern is analogous to a bridge passage in a classical sonata or an episode in a fugue. The player uses this rhythmic cliché as a sort of rest period to think out what style his next set of improvisations would take. In most ensembles of hourglass drums the rhythmic pattern at Figure 7 is invariably heard at one stage or the other. When the drum is played as a solo instrument for communication purposes. Drum rhythms in the northern part of Nigeria provide a different situation since all-drum orchestras are rare. A festival drum orchestra recorded by the author at Jos used three types of drums: *Kanango*, a high-pitch drum; *Kuntukuru*, a medium-pitch drum and *Dankaripi*, a small drum with a very piercing tone. The player of the *Kanango* also played the *Dankaripi* strapped to his leg producing this rhythm:

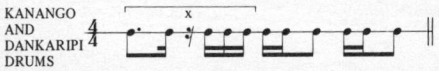

Figure 8.

A comparison between this rhythm and that produced by the *Ogaji* drum used to accompany a flute orchestra in Makurdi also in Northern Nigeria reveals a common pattern:

Figure 9.

The part marked **x** in both rhythms can be considered a standard rhythmic pattern frequently found in the instrumental music of the Hausas of Northern Nigeria. A rhythm similar to this is found in *Sakara* music of the Yorubas of Western Nigeria where a small drum shaped like a tambourine plays this rhythm:

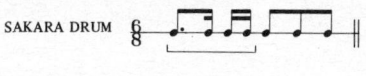

Figure 10.

A comparison between the rhythms of the *Koria* (calabash) drum of the Hausas and the *Kanango* (skin) drum of the Yorubas reveals an iambic pattern for the koria drum and a trochaic pattern for the kanango drum.

Figure 11.

Regional influences play a great part in the function of African instruments. The Kanango drum used by the Yorubas and Hausas are similar in construction but their functions and rhythmic patterns are vastly different.

Gong Rhythms

Dietz is of the opinion that 'gong-gongs are used as the foundation of the orchestra's background rhythm section throughout Africa. The iron gong is very important to the drum dance orchestra.'[1] The reference to drum orchestras is I think too far fetched and not borne out by facts. A correct way to put this would be to say that the bell rhythm which is the standard rhythm of the gong is found in almost all dance orchestras. It is not always played by the gong. King[2] tells us this rhythm is played by the *Kanango* drum of the Yorubas and in the music of the Ibibio people of South Eastern Nigeria, it is played by the woodblock. It can safely be said that most gong rhythms are variants of the bell rhythm as these transcriptions of gong rhythms from Nigeria show:

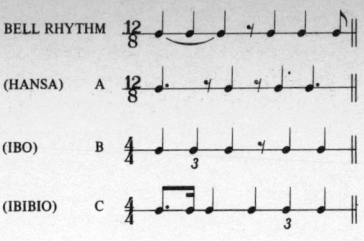

Figure 12.

The characteristics of the bell rhythm are evident at examples A, B and C which are variants of this rhythm. If there is a situation in which a gong can be considered very important, it is as an accompaniment to the voice rather than instruments where it is oftimes used instead of clapping or to punctuate incantations at a ritual ceremony. Nketia tells us that the Wagogo men of Tanzania 'generally prefer the accompaniment of idiophones where percussion accompaniment is desired'.[3]

A point worth noting about gong rhythms is that there are two types of gongs: conical gongs which produce only one tone and twin-gongs which are smaller in size and produce two tones tuned to the interval of a major second, a minor third or a perfect fifth. In Nigeria, the wooden drum which also produces two tones is tuned to the same intervals and these two instruments are used rhythmically to supply the inner voice-parts in an ensemble; an expert twin gong player knows how to exploit these two tones to the overall advantage of the ensemble.

References

[1] Betty Dietz and Michael Olatunji, *Musical Instruments of Africa* (New York: John Day Company, 1965), p. 44.

[2] Anthony King, *Yoruba Sacred Music from Ekiti* (Ibadan University Press, 1961), pp. 14–15.

[3] J. H. Nketia, 'The Instrumental Resources of African Music' (Institute of African Studies, Legon, Ghana, *Papers in African Studies*, n.d.), p. 2.

Chapter 6
The African Orchestra

An African orchestra is either used for ritual or nonritual purposes and the instrumentation in any given situation varies with the functions of the orchestra. It is rhythmically and melodically conceived in one of five ways: (1) All-drum orchestra, (2) Orchestra of drums plus other rhythmic instruments, (3) Orchestra of blowing instruments plus rhythm, (4) Orchestra of strings plus rhythm and (5) All-xylophone orchestra. In every combination, the range, pitch and individual characteristics of the instruments are taken into consideration before an ensemble is decided upon. Let us look more closely at these groupings.

All-Drum Orchestra
This is an orchestra of anything from two to six drums. Where there are only two players, the same type of drums, usually of the primary type, are used. The standard drum orchestra of four players comprises a soloist known as *mother drum* in many parts of Africa, a very high pitch drum and two medium-pitch drums. An orchestra of five drums usually employs a two-tone drum to strengthen the inner voice-parts; when more drums are used, they double the voices of the existing ones. The accent of a drum orchestra is strictly on rhythm producing polyrhythms which are a great feature of African music. With the exception of the soloist who is able to produce gradations of tone by playing his instrument with two hands, with one hand and a stick or two sticks, all the other drummers in an ensemble play strictly unvaried rhythmic patterns. From the figuration of each drum pattern, it is possible to deduce whether the music is produced by a large or small drum. In the following transcription of a drum orchestra from Eastern Nigeria, the solo drum's improvisations vary with every bar while the other instruments vary with every bar while the other

instruments maintain a steady rhythm. The medium pitched drum's rhythm is conceived in two-bar phrases and the small drum is content to emphasize the quarter notes of each bar.

Figure 1.

Orchestra of Drums plus Other Rhythmic Instruments

Sometimes more color is introduced into a drums ensemble by the addition of other rhythmic instruments like the gong, rattle or woodblock; the number of gongs, rattles or woodblocks used vary with different situations. This type of orchestra is strictly a nonritual one which can be used for dancing or other ceremonial occasions. The gong rhythmic pattern used is either the bell *rhythm* or its variant; and where a wooden drum is part of the ensemble, its two tones are used judiciously to fill in the inner-voices. Because of its hollow-sounding tones, a roll sounds better on the wooden drum that on a skin drum; the roll alternating with irregular staccato beats is a feature of the instrument. Great care is taken to see that the rhythmic figurations of a wooden drum and those of a large skin drum are clearly defined where both drums are present in an ensemble.

The *Etiliogu* orchestra of the Ibos (Figure 2) especially those from Udi town used to accompany the *Etiliogu* dance (wrongly called *Atilogu*), shows how a two-tone wooden drum is combined with a gong and a pot xylophone with two notes used rhythmically because of its limited melodic range. The rhythm of the pot xylophone is what identifies this orchestra.

Orchestra of Blowing Instruments plus Rhythm

The accent on this instrumentation is that of melodic improvisation supported by rhythm. It can take the form of a single melodic instrument supported by a drum or combination of melodic instruments supported by many rhythmic instruments. In the former case, the solo instrument, usually a flute of anything up to five stops, improvises freely over a steady drum rhythm as in the *Algaita* flute of the Hausas supported by a *Gangan* drum. In the latter case, three flutes

Etiliogu Orchestra

The signs (i) and (ii) show the two tones of the wooden drum

Figure 2.

join together to produce a melodic rhythm which is repeated over and over again with a fixed rhythmic drum support. A fine example of this is provided by the *Ogaki* (flute) ensemble of Nigeria whose three flutes are tuned to produce the notes of the pentatonic scale between them. The ensemble is supported by two drums called *Agaga* and *Ogaji*. The solo flutist is free to improvise over a resultant melodic rhythm produced by the other two flutes.

Where a solo flute with only two stops is used as is the case sometimes, the orchestra is conceived rhythmically rather than melodically; as in the case of the pot xylophone with two notes, the soloist plays the instrument rhythmically rather than melodically due to its limitations.

An orchestra of three flutes and two drums of the Tivs has this pattern:

Orchestra of Flutes and Drums

The resultant *melodic rhythm* produced by the second and third flute was this:

Figure 3.

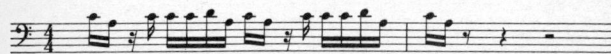

Figure 4.

The first flutists who was the soloist, improvised freely over this ostinato. There is a clear example of three-part counterpoint and harmonies in fourths, fifths and thirds.

Orchestra of Strings plus Rhythm

The only instance (apart from the Chopi musicians of Mozambique) where the skin drum is completely omitted from an African orchestra is where one or more stringed instruments are employed — and the reason is not far to seek. African harps and lutes are usually tuned rather low; and the sound of a one-string fiddle is not incisive enough to warrant the intrusion of a skin drum. Usually in a string orchestra, the player either accompanies himself or a soloist is introduced as vocalist. In its traditional setting in Nigeria, the orchestra is made up of three musicians — a string player, a vocalist and a third person playing the calabash drum with a light sharp tone. When the string instrument is a harp or lute, the musician plays an ostinato over which he sings softly. When it is a one-string fiddle, the melodic aspect is more emphasized and good players have been known to draw warm pentatonic melodies from their unsophisticated instruments with a frequent change of figuration as this transcription shows:

Melody by One-String Fiddle

Figure 5.

Even though it was possible for the fiddle to employ all the notes of a heptatonic scale, it was noticeable that the player only used the notes of the pentatonic scale. The rhythmical figurations of the *Koria* drum (chapter 4, figure 4) as an accompaniment to the *goge* fiddle, when compared with those of the typical Northern Nigerian drums (chapter 5, figures 8 and 9), show distinct regional characteristics. Sometimes instead of a *koria* drum, a two-stringed lute is accompanied by a bamboo (raft) zither, *ryomko*.

All-Xylophone Orchestra

This is an orchestra found only among the Chopi people of Mozambique.[1] It is a purely melodic orchestra perhaps the only instance in the whole of African music where melodic and contrapuntal patterns dominate rhythmic considerations.

There are certain instances, however, where anything up to three xylophones are played in conjunction with rhythmic instruments like the drum, gong, rattle and woodblock. The *Egwu Omaba* orchestra of the Ibos of Nsukka is perhaps unique in this respect. Three xylophones are used — one with four notes and two others with two notes all tuned to produce between them the notes of the pentatonic scale. Like the three-flute (*amada*) orchestra discussed earlier, the four-note xylophonists acts as soloist and the other two produce a melodic ostinato over which he improvises. The three xylophones produce this pattern:

Figure 6.

A small two-tone drum, rattle, gong and two high pitch drums are added to the ensemble to produce this overall result:

Egwu Omaba (Xylophone) Orchestra

Figure 7.

In actual performance, the instruments did not start all at once. It was necessary to have one instrument set the style and tempo so that the others could adapt their rhythmic figurations to this. The solo xylophonist started out first repeating the motive in the first measure a few times over to enable the other two xylophonists to join him contrapuntally and harmonically. After the three xylophonists had gotten their bearings, the other rhythmic instruments (starting with the gong) joined in with a steady rhythmic accompaniment which never varied throughout the performance.

References

[1] See Hugh Tracy, *Chopi Musicians: Their Music, Poetry and Instruments* (London: O.U.P., 1948).

Chapter 7
Anthropology of African Music

Anthropology we know to be a study of mankind; and social anthropology, with which we are concerned here, deals with the way people live together in organised societies. Mair tells us that 'a culture is the common possession of a body of people who share the same traditions in social terms. Such a body is a society'.[1] People who live in societies abide by certain traditions handed down through the years, which affect their behavioural patterns. One of these traditions is music; thus, when we talk of the anthropology of African Music, we are, in effect, referring to the way musical traditions affect the way of thinking and feeling of an African society.

Marriam feels that 'music exists only in terms of social interaction and it is learned behaviour... it involves the behviour of learned individuals and groups of individuals'.[2] But obviously because of their different environments, the African and the European conceive of music in different ways. According to Tracy, the word 'music' in Africa means 'vocal participation, the physical manipulation of instruments and the rhythmic or dance movements associated with music'.[3] To get at the true involvement of music in an African society, we have to study closely the role of music in religion, government and the various secret and ceremonial societies which regulate the lives of the people; not forgetting the individual and collective role of musical instruments.

From the day an African is born up to when he attains manhood, marries and eventually dies, music plays a very important part in his daily experiences. This will lead us to think that the behavioural patterns of a given society is to a large extent dependent on their musical concepts. The black man in Harlem who hears rock and roll music all day behaves quite differently from the black man who dances the samba in Brazil or to the black man in Mozambique who is motivated by the sweet sounds of his all-xylophone ensembles. As

Lomax puts it, music sound 'symbolises a fundamental and social-psychological pattern common to a given culture'.[4] In Nigeria, for example, you can differentiate an ethnic group, whether Yoruba, Ibibio, Hausa or Ibo by the type of rhythm they play. In general, complex music reflects a complex society and simple music a simple society. Music values are also reflective of general values. As a western trained musician, the writer's general values are different from those of his counterpart in a Nigerian village. What these values are and whether they are better or worse than those in the villages depends on the norms by which a given society lives. The music behaviour of a particular society causes them to react in a certain way. Concepts of music sound will determine the reaction of an audience to a performer in any African setting; this reaction is fed back to the performer who in turn reacts in a particular way.

Symbol and Rhythm

Musical symbols and rhythm contribute extensively to the African experience and state of well being. Rhythm is produced by musical instruments which function collectively as members of an ensemble or individually as symbols performing totally different functions. For example, in Tanzania a drum is hung on a tree when a young man is circumcised and taken down when he recovers; and in Ghana gourd rattles are carried to the market by maidens and shaken to attract the attention of eligible males. We also know that in certain parts of Ghana, the xylophone is played as a solo instrument to announce a death; and among the Hausa/Fulanis of Nigeria, a two-stringed lyre *Giraya* is played for a woman who dances until she gets into a fit. The player is usually approached by a woman who pays a little sum of money and asks for a particular music to be played for her. She dances alone to this music which gets wilder and wilder until she goes into a fit. She is revived by water being poured over her and leaves very satisfied by the experience — a very good example of music and behaviour in an African society.

Examples of musical instruments as symbols abound in the music of the Nigerian people. In Northern Nigeria, when an Emir enters or leaves his palace the sound of the *Kakaki*, elongated metal trumpets, can be clearly heard. Elephant tusks are carried by royalty as a symbol of power and played on ad libitum; all of which goes to fortify Lomax's view quoted earlier that music sound 'symbolises a social-psychological pattern common to a given culture'.

Number symbolism in African music is a subject sadly neglected by research scholars; and yet this features very prominently in ritual ceremonies and instrumentation in traditional orchestras. From

Nigerian experiences, we find the numbers 3, 4 and 7 occuring so often in instrumentations and rituals to lead us to believe that they are of great cultural significance. Among the Yorubas *four* drums are used for the worship of the god of creation, Obatala — Iya Nla, Iya Agan, Afere and Keke; during the Ofala festival at Onitsha as Marius Nkwoh tells us,[5] *four* drums — Ozi, Idah, Kpikili and Nwoke are featured prominently. Along the Ibibios, *four* horns — Eka, Uta, Akpan Uta, Udo Utah and Etukudo Uta are used in an ensemble of seven musicians.[6] In the worship of the god Sango, the Yorubas use *four* drums — Iya Ilu Bata, Emele Ako, Emele Abo and Kudi. The Biroms of Northern Nigeria use *four* transverse flutes made of bamboo in their *kara* flute ensemble. The Ebre women's secret society of the Ibibios used *three* gongs in their instrumental ensemble; and to be inititated into the Ekpo secret society of the Ibibios, *seven* circles are drawn on the ground and the novitiate is made to step into each of the circles. There is a belief among some sections of the Nigerian community that the number 4 represents male, the number 3 female and the number 7 a mixture of male and female (4+3). This thesis has not been conclusively proven; but it is significant that among the Ibibios, Efiks and Ekois and in some parts of Arochuku in Ibo country, men and women are initiated in to the *Ekpo* society which uses the number 7 very prominently in its initiation process (4+3).

In all the drum and flute ensembles mentioned above, rhythm plays a very prominent part. You differentiate one drum orchestra from another by the rhythms each group plays; and this in turn is tied to the traditional pattern of worshipping a particular ancestral god. Rhythm leads to movement, making the dance patterns used in ritual worship of special significance to initiated members of a secret society.

Song Texts as Culture Indicators

In African music, song texts can act as historical commentaries or culture indicators. For example the *Oriki* music of the Yorubas is a form of historical commentary; and African historians trained in the western idiom are more and more beginning to take a closer look at these oral masterpieces which used to be taken purely at their face value as nothing more than entertainment. A thorough examination of song texts will prove that they serve special functions; and function, we know, constrains form, since the form of a piece of music is dictated by the use to which it is put. Song texts can also be used as birds of passage; they can be set to different kinds of music to meet the required needs of the singer. Before an *Mbopo* or fattening room ceremony of the Ibibios, a clitoridectomy is performed on the virgin about to be initiated. During the painful operation without anesthetic, a band of musicians gather round to play and sing in order to drown her cries of pain as she is supposed to undergo the operation in silence; perhaps a good example of *gebrauchs-musik* in an African setting. Like rhythm, the complexity of a song also reflects a complex society; song texts are an adaptation of the traits of a given society and they have been know to diffuse from the cultures of one society to that of another. The social structure of a society can affect the style of a song; and this structure can either be stratified or egalitarian.

Songs of social control are usually topical and appropriate to a given community; they are either of praise or abuse designed to regulate the social order. Sometimes they are philosophical and humourous since the African's sense of humour is best expressed in song and proverbs. Songs of social control with their carefully worded texts, often serve as a village newspaper expanding on important happenings in the daily life of the society — the beautiful girl in the village who is promiscuous; the ageing woman who marries a man many years her junior; the lady chorister caught in the pastor's bedroom; the prominent man in the village who is an élite by day but an armed robber at night.

If you watch a group of Africans pushing a truck full of heavy merchandise or making a clearing in the bush with their cutlasses, you will find yet another example of rhythm helping to ease the burden of the labour in the form of work songs since the metronome sense is never absent from the spirit of the African.

Music in Secret Societies

Janheinz Jahn tells us that 'in traditional African culture, all life is based on religion'.[7] He was stretching a valid point rather too far; but there is no getting away from the fact that traditional religious beliefs or what western scholars call secret societies, controlled and regulated many African societies. The efficacy of these societies which waned considerably with the advent of Christianity and Islamism, has been revived with the current cultural awakening sweeping through the African continent possibly because 'in African religion which is man centred, man has an active attitude towards the gods. Through the sympathetic magic invocation he compels the divine power to unite him in ecstasy'.[8]

Among the Ibibios of Nigeria, all ritual cermonies in honour of their supreme being, Abasi is called *Mbre Idem* — musical ceremony of the ancestral spirits; in other words, the whole act of ancestral worship unites the African with his gods in ecstasy and is principally music orientated. Wissler lists five major events which take place in a ritualistic ceremony as 'impersonation of mythical being, songs, dances, definite equipment and proscribed series of manipulations'.[9]

In the African experience, impersonation of mythical beings takes the form of masquerades speaking in falsetto voices to represent the gods; definite equipment can take the form of standard instrumentation in orchestral ensembles and the proscribed series of manipulations includes sacrifices to the gods.

This leaves us with *song and dance* which are perhaps the most important part of the ceremony. Songs and dances are introduced into secret societies because humans belong to movement and speech communities; dancing employs cultural patterns found in other behaviours typical of a given community; and songs are important because according to Wissler, 'the greatest magical power resides in song'.[10] Dancing involves movement and in the case of the African, vigorous movement; and Dalcrose feels that 'bodily movements awaken images in the mind. The stronger the muscular sensations, the clearer and more precise the image... feeling is born of sensation'.[11]

Let us take a look at the use of song and dance in one or two Nigerian societies. During the Iju Festival performed at the death of a chief in Okitipupa, the ritual ceremony consists of a call to worship (where drums are used), incantation, dance with a sword and finale. The Ogboni and Egungun cults of the Yorubas have masquerades like *Ode, Alagbo, Sembe* and *Arebe* where singing and dancing include circus-like tricks. The *Eyo* masquereade of the Yorubas and *Ekpo Ndok* masquerade of the Ibibios have as their main theme dancing and entertainment as they move about the streets to the delight of the spectators. Giones sees African music functioning 'as part of religious ritual, as an expression of social organisation and as recreation'.[12] The recreational aspect of ritual societies is often overlooked in musical and anthropological studies and too often more attention is focused on the rites of a ritual society to the detriment of musical content which is sometimes of greater importance.

In religious ritual, African musical instruments fulfil not only rhythmic and melodic functions, but anthropological ones as well. In one Nigerian community, six *Lera* flutes are played at the installation of a chief with the head chief of the community playing the leading flute himself. The question of whether he is the best flute player available to lead the group does not necessarily arise as his presence in the gorup is symbolic of authority rather than musical competence. The whole ceremony would be meaningless without this single musical gesture. In African music, music sound is as important, and sometimes even more important than the musical instrument producing the sound. Among the Ibibios, the sound of a twin gong (*Akankan*) played solo in a village, tells the people that an official announcement is about to be made. Also, the sound of *Uta* horns alerts the people that either a prominent woman has summoned the musicians to her place to play in order to revitalise her waning youthful powers. Either way, the sound of the horns at once awakens in the listener images of a woman, dead or alive.

The quartet of *Uta* horns, as we have already seen, is named after a woman and her three sons. The reason for an ageing woman summoning *uta* musicians to invoke the spirits to give her back her youthful powers is not unconnected with the tradition of the Ibibios that male children are more important than females. This tradition also holds in many African countries where a woman is not regarded as really important until she has delivered a male child. As Turner tells us 'ritual symbolism can only flourish where there is a thriving corporate life. The symbols are related to the process of adjusting the individual to the traditional social order in which he was born'.[13]

References

[1] Lucy Mair, An Introduction to Social Anthropology (Oxford: The Clarendon Press, 1965), p. 8.

[2] Alan Merriam, *The Anthropology of Music* (Evanston: Northwestern University Press, 1964), p. 27.

[3] Hugh Tracy, *African Music — Codification and Textbook Project* (Roodepoort, Transvaal, South Africa), p. 10.

[4] Alan Lomax, 'Folk Song Style' (*American Anthropologist*, 61), p. 950.

[5] Marius Nkwo, 'The Great Ofala' (*Nigeria Magazine*, Nos. 110–112, 1974), p. 6.

[6] See, Samuel Ekpe Akpabot, *Ibibio Music in Nigerian Culture* (East Lansing: Michigan State University Press, 1975), pp. 53–58.

[7] Janheinz Jahn, *Neo-African Literature — A History of Black Writing*, trans: Oliver Coburn and Ursula Lehrburger (New York: Grove Press Inc, 1968), p. 157.

[8] *Ibid*, p. 158.

[9] Clark Wissler, *An Introduction to Social Anthropology* (New York: Henry Holt and Company, 1929), pp. 265–284.

[10] *Ibid*, p. 278.

[11] Emile Jaques Dalcrose, *Rhythm, Music and Education* (New York: G. P. Putnam and Sons, The Knickerbocker Press, 1921), p. 124.

[12] Leonard Giones, 'Music of Africa South of the Sahara' (*Music Educator's Journal*, Vol. 59, 1972), p. 48.

[13] V. W. Turner, *The Drums of Affliction* (Oxford: Clarendon Press, 1968), p. 22.

Chapter 8
Random Music in Nigeria

Nigerian flutes as we have seen generally come in two varieties: those with two to three stops which play melodic rhythms and others with five stops which are capable of playing short melodies. With the possible exception of *Lere* flutes of the Yorubas, flutes capable of producing distinctive melodies are found in the Northen parts of the country. In areas where there have been constant movement of traders from south to north like Gboko which separates the Ibos from the Tivs, the flutes called *Amada* have only three stops; but unlike the Ibo flute, *Oja* which is played singly, *Amada* flutes are used in groups of three using the hocket technique to produce a melody. Further up in the land of the Tivs in Makurdi, where the people interact regularly with the Hausas, there is the five-tone flute called *Ityam* which functions like the Hausa *Algaita*.

Nigerian flutes are usually made of wood; but the Edos, famous for their carving skills, have been able to fashion their instruments from bronze or carved out of the teeth of large wild animals like the boar. All the flutes mentioned are used for festival and dance music except the Lere flutes which have ritualistic associations. Almost all the flutes found in Nigeria are vertical flutes; the author did not come across any examples of transverse flutes in his research.

In the *Atilogwu* dance of the Ibos discussed in chapter 6, we have to point out that the word *Atilogwu* is a corruption of the word *Etiliogwu* which in Ibo means 'is it magic?'; this is because of the simultaneous rhythmic figurations of the large gong *Alo* in the orchestra with the dance steps of the group it accompanies, which was seen by the spectators as being magical in execution. The melody or melodic rhythm produced by the *Amada* flutes of the Tivs on transcription was found to be pointillistic in conception probably because the three flutes uesed were tuned to different pitches.

All the flutes so far mentioned are direct contrasts to the situation in Ghana where Nketia tell us that 'the flute Anadwo Sekan is played during stool ceremonies, particularly those of the annual festival'.[2] With this background knowledge of the general organisation of Nigerian flute ensembles, the *Kara* (or *Busa*) flute ensemble of the Birom people of Northern Nigeria is of special musical interest. *Kara* is a transverse flute made of bamboo with three of four stops played orchestrally in groups of four with a small drum called *Ganga*[3] as accompaniment. An analysis of this group shows this to be an example of random or chance music in Nigeria. Most of the orchestral ensembles we have come across so far, have operated under the general of a group of instruments providing a steady unvarying rhythm with a soloist improvising over this. But with the *Kara* ensemble it was different.

Talking of interderminacy in random music, Cage writes:

'In the case, however, of the performance of music the composition of which is indeterminate of its performance so that the action of the players is productive of a process, no harmonious fusion of sound is essential. A non-obstruction of sounds is of the essence.'[4]

This is exactly what happens in *Kara* music. The whole performance is a process; it is indeterminate; and the sounds produced by the players are not obstructed by a conscious attempt to organize the rhythms and harmonies. John Cage was obviously discovering in the thirties what indigeneous African musicians had been practising since antiquity. A closer look at the organization of this orchestra might perhaps help to provide the student of aleatoric music with a natural example of what constitutes this type of music composition as opposed to the conceived randomness of Cage, Stockhausen or Dallapiccola. The four *kara* flutes were found to be tuned to the pentatonic scale:

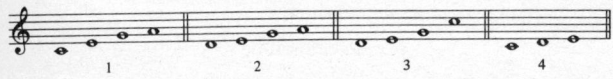

Figure 1.

The notes of the flutes sounded rather muffled and it seemed there was a definite attempt by the players to 'blue' the notes instead of playing them cleanly. Although each instrument had only two stops, the players were able to produce up to four notes by a special lip action much in the manner of European clarino players of the 17th and 18th centuries.

To start the performance, first one player and then another started playing at random. There was no signal given or implied; each player just came in when he felt like it and stopped playing briefly at random to take a breath, blow his nose or even urinate in a nearby bush. Sometimes an argument of some sort developed between two players and as they argued, the other players continued playing completely oblivious to their bickering with the *ganga* drum beating out improvised tatoos. Such a scene is absolutely impossible to notate effectively.

The common process in African instrumental ensembles is either to use the technique of call-and-response or to build up an ostinato over which a soloist improvises. There is always an element of organization in the whole proceeding. With the Kara flute ensemble, the technique was vastly different. All the instruments were treated as equal partners and each one was free to improvise at liberty producing something like this:

Kara Flute Ensemble

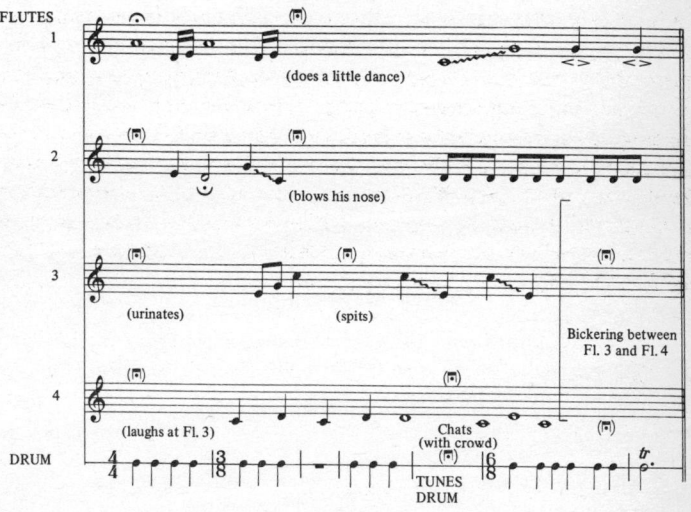

Figure 2.

The result was random counterpoint in four parts in which dissonance featured freely producing an eerie feeling suggestive of background music for a film about a killer stalking his victim in a haunted house. The function of the *ganga* drum was also of very special interest. Generally in African instrumental music, we conceive the drum as supplying strict rhythm or improvised rhythm within a consistent rhythm ostinato. Here it was different. The *ganga* drum provided a kind of polyrhythmic *recitativo secco* which punctuated the improvisation of the four soloists. When it was time to end the performance, the players just quit one by one at random until it was obvious there was nothing more to listen to.

Many of the elements of twentieth century music after 1918 were present in the music of the *Kara* orchestra.[5] The tone clusters and the harmony created by the individual melodic lines of Bartok; the random approach of Cage; the special effects of Dallapiccola; the polyrhythms of Stravinsky; the distorted tones of Boulez. In an interview with the musicians, it was established that *Kara* music can be played for a happy or sad occsion. During a happy occasion like a birth or wedding, the players tended to use notes of short duration; on sad occasions like a death, the notes tended to be longer in value and more sustained producing sustained dissonance which tended to highlight the anguish of the occasion.

Obviously program is another feature of Kara music; only in this instance, each player is free to express the pain or joy he feels. These are all put together to produce a unique African musical experience.

References

[1] For a discussion on Nigerian flute orchestras, see Samuel Akpabot, *Instrumentation in African Music* (Unpublished Fellowship Thesis, Trinity College of Music, London, 1967), pp. 62-91.

[2] J. H. Kwabena Nketia, 'The Instrumental Resources of African Music', *Papers in African Studies*, Institute of African Studies, Legon, Ghana, p. 21.

[3] Not to be confused with the general name *gangan* given to all hourglass talking drums of the Yorubas of Western Nigeria.

[4] John Cage, *Silence* (Middleton, Connecticut: Wesleyan University Press, 1939), p. 39.

[5] The author has used many elements of twentieth century notation to transcribe this recording from Jos which describes the music adequately.

Chapter 9
Notation, Terminology and Legends

Notation

It is the view of this author that many problems concerning African music have been exaggerated to such proportions as to make them appear insoluble. In fact the problems can be divided into two: (a) those facing a western scholar trying to understand the music of Africa, (b) those facing anyone trying to transcribe and measure this music. For many years it was left to western musicologists, anthropologists and sociologists to explain the music of Africa to the world; they did a good job and laid some foundations for future research. Today the situation is different. Africans with training comparable to western researchers are now re-discovering and writing about this music free from many of the problems that confronted early western scholars.

One example will perhaps make this point clearer. Jones in a pioneering work on African music, quoted in chapter three, was of the opinion that the factors which determine a speech melody leap remain to be discovered. He had a little problem here which does not exist with an African who speaks the language from which the speech melody evolves; the African just says the sentence correctly and the melody becomes clearly outlined in the process. For instance the Ibibios of Nigeria call a twin gong A-kang-kang; if we notate this sound it will be something like this:

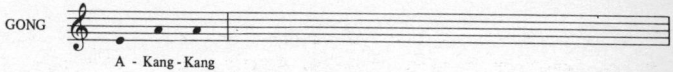

Figure 1.

A perfect fourth. If you reduce or increase this interval, the word assumes a different meaning or no meaning at all. The story is told of an English missionary who was preaching to a Nigerian congregation and wanted to say 'God is strength' in the Ibo language — *Chineke bu ike*. Everytime he said this, his audience laughed and he could not understand what the joke was all about. Eventually he learned that what he was saying was 'God is buttocks'; the word *Ike* could either mean *strength* or *buttocks* depending on its inflection.

Anyone trying to notate African rhythms must have come across certain parts that seemed to defy conventional notation. The tendency in these cases is either to try and employ elaborate western metric notations to solve the problem, or propound yet another dubious theory on African rhythms. But let us look at the problem once again. Surely in the waltzes of Chopin we find instances of elaborate metric figurations which we solve; in the Spanish piano music of Albenitz and Granados we find many instances of notes interpreted slightly differently from how they are written; why then should the rhythms in African music be viewed differently?

Any dance band musician will tell you that when he plays a rhumba he is not playing the notes rigidly as written but interpreting them. This is exactly what happens in some African instrumental music; but strangely enough many scholars trying to notate this music want to get everything into their transcription which is sometimes impossible.

It is the opinion of the author that three Greek rhythmic modes permiate all African music: the imabic mode (u —); the trochaic mode (— u) and the spondee mode (— —); these three are all combined in the *bell rhythm* of the gong:

Figure 2.

If a researcher get these three rhythms firmly established in his mind before setting out to transcribe African melodies he will most certainly find his task much easier than trying to use symbols and a clever manipulation of notes and meter which in the end expresses more than the indigeneous African musicians intended. It is the experience of the author that triple time-figures are very strong in African music but agrees with Ward[1] that 'the underlying percussion rhythm makes it quite clear that the African feels it is duple time'.

Another notational problem commonly found in the transcription of African rhythms is that of bar lines. In any given ensemble where the instruments are playing strict rhythm, there should be no problem determining the meter of each instrumental pattern from the *tactus*.

The problem comes when one tries to transcribe the free improvisation of a master drummer within a strict rhythmic framework; surely this is not more impossible than trying to notate the free improvisation of 'bop' chorus by Charlie Parker or Dizzy Gillespie. The African and western experiences here are similar and it is not advancing the cause of scholarship to suggest that there are any hidden difficulties existing in the African music transcription that do not exist in a Charlie Parker transcription. One subtle difference could be in the way both solos are conceived. Jazz is essentially a 'four to the bar' style of music no matter many modern attempts to make it sound otherwise. African music is also similarly conceived but with very strong triple-time associations.

One point frequently neglected in the transcription of African rhythms concerns the two tones produced by instruments like the wooden gong, two-tone drum, pot drum or twin-gong in an ensemble. The two tones of the pot drum are muffled as are those of the twin-skin drum; but those of the wooden drum and gong produce intervals of a major second, minor third and perfect fifth depending on the size of the instrument. Let us consider this rhythmic pattern:

Figure 3.

This rhythm can be clapped or tapped on a table; but when played by the wooden drum, twin-gong, pot drum or two-tone skin drum the notation becomes different and the figuration assumes colouristic overtones.

Figure 4.

The figures (i) and (ii) refer to the notation for the low and high tones produced by the instruments. Where single line is used in the transcription, it implies that there is no tonal change in the rhythmic figuration; in the case of the pot drum, it indicates that the two tones produced are muffled. The transcription of the twin-gong pattern tells us that it is an instrument with two tones a second apart; and that of the wooden drum that its two tones are a fifth apart. Sometimes, as in the music of the Ibibio people of Nigeria, two wooden drums are used in an ensemble tuned to intervals of a minor third and a perfect fifth. If the rhythm in Figure 3 were to be played in these two drums in an orchestra it would be transcribed as follows:

Figure 5.

It is assumed that in picking the wooden drums, the musicians make sure (as they always do) that one tone is common to both instruments. The old impression that African music is rhythm and melody is erroneous as modern research has shown. Many things happening in the inner-voices are as important as the melodic and rhythmic elements.

Terminology

Because of the hundreds of languages spoken in Africa, one instrument can have as many as ten names. The names *Sanza, Mbira, Ubo Aka, Ikpa Mboto, Agidigbo, Kembe*, refer to an instrument known by westerners as kaffir piano, hand piano, thumb piano or finger xylophone. All these names are most confusing and the frivolous manner in which some African musical instruments are sometimes alluded to is in part responsible for the 'carefree' way in which many people treat them. The author is here suggesting that the *Sanza* be known universally as *thumb piano* as this reflects its heptatonic scale which is very close to the diatonic scale of the piano, and the fact that it is played only with the thumbs.

Reference has been made in these pages to the *wooden drum* which is sometimes wrongly described as a slit drum or wooden gong. Andrew Tracy, Editor of *African Music*, in a discussion with the author suggests that *wood drum* might be a better name since the instrument is made of wood — in the same way as we say skin drum and calabash drum to label drums covered with skin or carved out of a calabash. One is tempted to go along with Mr. Tracy, although the name *wooden drum* has been in use for so long that it has become a standard name for the instrument. This instrument is not a slit drum or a wooden gong which are both very poor descriptions. Every drum made of wood is either hollowed or slit; and a gong in African music refers specifically to a metal instrument. Some writers have even gone as far as referring to a gong as a metal clanger; following this line of reasoning, we might as well refer to the woodblock as a wooden clanger since the instrument is struck in exactly the same way as the gong, but this would be incorrect.

A terminology frequently encountered is *talking drum*, used to describe the large solo drum in an ensemble; but we know that all drums used in African music talk. The hourglass drum talks, the pot drum talks, the calabash drum talks and the wooden drum talks; the difference between them is in what they say and the way they say it. The wooden drum with two tones talks more elequently than the pot drum which also has two tones; and the hourglass drum produces more gradations of color in its speech than the calabash drum with its dry sound. It is here being suggested that future researchers use the terminology *talking drums* to refer to African drums collectively and identify any drum under discussion specifically by name; in this way any looseness in terminology will be avoided.

In describing the concerto grosso of the Baroque period, reference is frequently made to *repieno and concertante* or *solo and tutti* to describe a small group of instruments contrasted with a large group. Since the same compositional process occurs in African music except that the style and setting is different, then the term *call-and-response* should be a standard one when referring to the antiphonal style of African vocal music; and *cantor and chorus* should be synonymous with *solo and tutti*. In this way these expressions will be standardized, making their use in the instruction of African music in schools more uniform. African music terminology should be able to make use of world music terminology where applicable or identifiable with it where strictly impossible to do so.

It is strange how we use the expressions *polyrhythms* and *polymeters* when referring to some western music and immediately change these to 'cross rhythms' and 'clash or rhythms'[2] when talking about African music, where in fact these rhythms more commonly exist; in which case why introduce new terminology when the established ones will do? The point being made here is that African music should be viewed in the same light as English music or German music or Italian music;

each type of music possessing special characteristics which together form world music. Expressions like 'exotic' used to describe African music only tend to make researchers and students approach the subject with a wariness which leads to misleading conclusions.

Discussing the thumb piano used by the Gonja people of Ghana, Mensah[3] transcribes a passage using the pentatonic scale and notes that it is

> '... so near the scale obtained from the black notes of the pianoforte that the ear trained in European classical music tends to equate the two. But instant minute intervallic differences indicate that the Gonja scale is not to be identified with any western penta forms.'

Figure 6.

A close look at Mensah's transcription above will fail to detect any 'instant minute intervallic differences' between the notes. The passage is clearly in the pentatonic scale — the intervals from A to C forming an anhemitonic pentatonic scale on a tonic C; and to suggest any hidden meaning is to help to perpetuate the myths of African music.

There are always intervallic differences in transcriptions of African music because the scales are not of equal temperament as in western music; this is why we talk of the heptatonic scale when referring to African music as opposed to the diatonic scale of western music, even though notes of the two scales sound more or less the same. Here is a transcription of the notes of a six-tone wooden drum called *Lukumbi* used by the Batetela people of Central Zaire:

Figure 7.

The intervallic differences ranging from one to two tones are clearly notated and can actually be played on a keyboard instrument. Tracy counsels that

> '....it is advisable for a research musician when first encountering a strange music to rationalize about it as if he intended to play the music himself and not only to comment upon it.'[4]

Books on African musical instruments do not seem to agree on the differences between a trumpet, horn and flute; but yet in the mind of the indigeneous African musican these instruments are clearly identified. In western music, the sounds of the flute, horn and trumpet are distinct — but so are the sounds of these instruments in their African context if a researcher cares to differentiate them. Trumpets are usually made of metal or wood; flutes from bamboo reeds and sometimes wood, and horns from the antennae of animals, the tusk of elephants and gourds.

The sound of an African horn is not unlike that of a western horn with the same dark quality reminiscent of the call of the wild. Trumpets are what their name implies — brassy in tone when made of metal and only less so when made of wood with a brass mouthpiece, flutes have a reedy piercing sound which is unmistakable. With all these obvious characteristics, one wonders why we should be talking about 'elephant tusk trumpets'. Dietz and Olatunji write that 'horns and trumpets... are commonly made from the tusks and horns of animals'.[5] This is not correct. Trumpets are never made from the tusks and horns of animals — only horns are. For an African aerophone to qualify as a trumpet, it must have a mouthpiece; otherwise it is either a horn or a flute. To qualify as a flute, it must have at least two stops and its sounds controlled by the movement of the fingers as distinct from the lip and palm control which is characteristic of horns. By making these clear distinctions, a student of African music will be able to clearly conceptualize what a particular instrument looks and sounds like instead of being given the impression that in this type of music anything goes; and that trumpets, horns and flutes are to all intents and purposes the same. They are not, as their functions show. An elephant tusk horn is only played *by* royalty whereas a brass trumpet is played *for* royalty; a wooden trumpet on the other hand is played at the funeral of an elderly person in the community.

Legends and Myths

In the chapter on 'Theories on African Music', Tracy has rightly stated that the attribute 'African' in any discussion of African music evokes a sinister 'abstract'. This sinister approach to the problem is what has greatly hindered a wider understanding and acceptance of African music in its true form. The author remembers vividly his first African music class at Michigan State University in 1973. He was beseiged by students who wanted to enroll for the course asking questions like, 'Is it very difficult?' or 'They tell me African music is really weird' or 'Are you going to tell us about the "voodoo" associated with this type of music?' These questions were only representative of the 'sinister abstracts' that these students, many of them versed in the ways of western musci, imagined existed in African music.

Halfway through the course, two students came to complain that 'all these facts are making it difficult for us to enjoy the music; is it possible for you to cut out all the terminologies and just teach us some songs and clap patterns so that we can teach them to our grade schoolchildren?' The attitude of these students is typical of the attitude of many western researchers into African music. Let us look at some of these myths and legends.

The Yorubas of Nigeria believe that only trees located near the roadside are suitable materials for the construction of skin drums because they overhear humans conversing as they walk past and are therefore able to reproduce their language. The Ghanaians forbid a master drummer to carry his drum on his head as this could lead to disastrous results; it has to be carried for him by an assistant. The phallic symbol has been introduced into the music of the wooden drum by writers who claim that the opening in the drum represents a naked woman and the two mallets used to strike the instrument are men making love to her. This statement is as ridiculous as saying that the large open end of a French horn is a woman and the hand that a player inserts into it to hold the instrument firmly, is a man making love to it. If one 'theory' about African music is true, then surely the other must be true also for Africans are not the only people who make love.

Tracy probably had this erroneous approach to African music in mind when he writes that:

> 'The success of the Project will be in direct proportion to the degree in which instrinsically African musical forms are logically conceptualized, and thus expressed in clearly understood literate terms which can be compared with musical phenomena elsewhere without the implication of extraneous or derogatory standards of judgement.'[6]

Many times erroneous theories on African music are expounded by researchers who believe myths and legends about African people so firmly that they refuse to accept the fact that sounds they are hearing can sometimes be equated with concepts of western music practices. Take the question of harmonic concepts in African music for an example. Hornbostel[7] believes that there is no harmony in African music only '*organum* in parallel motion which represents a primitive stage of polyphony... this kind of polyphony has nothing to do with harmony as we understand it.' Ward[8] takes an opposite view by stating that 'fourths and fifths seem never to be consecutive and fifths are rare altogether.' Jones[9] is of the opinion that 'part of the crowd sings the tune and part of the crowd sings the same tune a 4th or a 5th below.' The experience of this author is that the harmony of the Ibibio people of Nigeria is most frequently in fourths and fifths producing organum in parallel motion. Waterman[10] talks of a *bias* (this author prefers the word *myth*) against African music by researchers of a decade or two ago who 'transcribed African music without ever hearing harmony used, even though harmony may actually have been present.'

Hornbostel wrote in 1928, Ward in 1927, Jones in 1956, Waterman in 1952. Examining all these diverse opinions on the same subject, is it any wonder that the average man or woman gets very confused whenever the subject of African music is raised? The bias that Waterman talks about is actually the myth or sinister abstract about African music expressed in another way. The experiences of this author in 1975 regarding the points raised by musicologists of the twenties and fifties based upon a continuing research into Nigerian music can be summed up in this way:

(a) Harmony, as westerners conceive it, is present in African music although this is sometimes improvisatory rather than pre-conceived.

(b) Preconceived harmony exists in fourths and fifths in the style of strict *organum*.

(c) The musicians deliberately sing the same melody a fourth or fifth below to produce harmony.

(d) African harmony and polyphony separately conceived.

Merriam[11] thinks 'it is doubtful that the African viewpoint would make a distinction between concepts of vertical and horizontal music structure.' This author has been present at many rehearsals by Nigerian traditional singing groups free from western influences and heard arguments among the musicians like:

(1) 'You are singing my part; sing your own part.'
(2) 'You cannot come in until the other singer has done so.'
(3) 'That part you are singing is not sounding right.'
(4) 'Let us hear the words of the cantor; don't come in whenhe is singing.'

Clearly (1) is an obvious reference to a harmonic conception. (2) has contrapuntal overtones, (3) is a reference to the type of harmony being supplied and (4) deals with the style of call-and-response and improvisatory counterpoint synonymous with African vocal music.

These observations are possible because this author speaks the language of the group he was observing and was able to pick up some information at rehearsals that do not surface at actual performances.

One of the difficulties that western researchers face is that the African musician likes to put on a show whenever there are strangers around, but, more and more African musicologists are being trained in the ways of western musical scholarship and using this knowledge to take another look at the indigenous music of their countries. Current research into African traditional music, has revealed many unfortunate distortions of facts by some writers on the subject. These distortions, according to Mantle Hood, are caused by lack of sufficient knowledge of all the conditions that influence African musical practices.[12] They could also be caused by faulty pre-conceived ideas and European bias on events in Africa, which we know dies very hard. While it is true that western scholars pioneered the study of African music, it is also true that they must be prepared now to listen to the voice of African scholars talking about the music of their people from the grass roots and disagreeing, sometimes painfully, with some conclusions that have held sway for many years. This is the only way in which the horizons of African music can be widened.

References

[1] W. E. Ward, 'Music in the Gold Coast' (*Gold Coast Review* III, July-December, 1927), pp. 219-220

[2] A. M. Jones, 'African Rhythm' (*Africa*, XXIV, January, 1954), pp. 26-27.

[3] A. A. Mensah, 'The Gyilo — A Gonja Sansa' (*Paper in African Studies*), p. 39.

[4] Hugh Tracy, *African Music — Codification and Textbook Project* (Tansvaal, The International Library of African Music, June 1969), p. 11.

[5] Betty Diaz and Michael Olatunji, *Musical Instruments of Africa* (New York: The John Day Company, 1965), p. 64.

[6] Hugh Tracy, op. cit. p. 10.

[7] E. M. Hornbostel, 'African Negro Music' (*Africa*, Vol. 1, 1928), pp. 13-15.

[8] W. E. Ward, op. cit. p. 213.

[9] A. M. Jones, *Studies in African Music* (London: OUP, 1956), p. 12.

[10] Richard A. Waterman, 'African Influence on the Music of the Americas', (*Acculturation in the Americas*, Sol. Tax ed Vol. 11, Univeristy of Chicago Press, 1952), pp. 208-209.

[11] Alan Merriam, 'African Music' (*Continuity and Change in African Cultures*, William R. Bascom and Melville J. Herskovits ed. University of Chicago Press, 1959), p. 78.

[12] See Mantle Hood, 'Musical Significance' (*Ethnomusicology*, V11/3, 1963), pp. 187-192.

Chapter 10
Traditional Africa Music Elements in Twentieth Century Western Music

In its traditional setting, African music is not written down. In conception and performance, it is an oral tradition handed down from generation to generation and jealousy preserved by those who have come to be known as master musicians. The purest form of this music is found in ritualistic ceremonies where a strict format in instrumentation and ancestral-worship patterns is maintained. This is opposed to music for social occasions, where there is flexibility in instrumentation and performance practices: here we find that no two performances are exactly the same because of the improvisatory element consistently present in the totality of the presentation.

It is the opinion of the author that music used for ritual or ancestral worship forms the basis of *African Classical music*. Any other form of African music at one time or the other suffers from acculturation because the ceremonies are not limited to initiated members of a particular secret society.[1] The rhythms, symbols and songs used in ritualistic ceremonies are standard and not subject to change or experiments.

Because African music is not written down, European composers with sophisticated equipment and a tradition of notated music, have been able to get honourable mention in books on music history as innovators or inventors of musical styles that have existed in Africa for centuries. Our aim here is to take a close look at some twentieth century western music practices that have existed in the African continent for years. It is hoped that this will cause the writers of future music history books to re-assess their primary sources which can many times be traced to Africa. Let us take a look at some of these practices.

Random Music

We have in our discussion on Nigerian Random Music (chapter 8) quoted John Cage's view on the action of players which is productive of a process and indeterminate of a performance. In order that the author's views in this chapter can be seen as a corporate whole, we will restate some observations from that specific study of Birom random music. Cage was writing about change music which he, Stockhausaen and Dallapicola, among others are credited with having innovated. But the evidence we have come across, shows clearly that what Cage was trying to explain in 1939, had been practiced by Nigerian musicians for centuries before that time. On a research tour to Northern Nigeria, the author was amazed to find a group of five musicians — four flute players and a drummer — playing random music that came naturally to them. The difference between what these musicians were playing at Jos in Nigeria and what Cage was trying to play at a concert in New York, was that one was spontaneous and the other, *stage managed*. Cage and the African musicians were all exploring time and space in music; but whereas Cage had to sit down and work it all out, these magnificent musicians from Nigeria played the music almost instinctively. The result was that the Cage performance was wooden and tended to make the audience laugh or become bewildered; but the African performance so blended with its natural environment, that there was nothing artificial about the group; not even when the one of the musicians walked away to urinate, or two flautists started arguing while the others played on oblivious of their bickering.

During the performance, one or other of the musicians did a little dance, blew his nose, laughed, spat or had a little chat with the audience. At first contact, the author found the whole experience very unusual; and it took some time to realise that this was perhaps the truest form of aleatoric music. When the musicians played again, the performance was slightly different in style but still retained the framework of chance or randomness; there was no signal given for the musicians to start playing and none to stop. The instrumentation was made up of four side blown flutes made from bamboo called *kara* supported by a *gangan* drum. The tones of the flutes sounded rather muffled and it seemed there was a definite attempt by the players to 'blue' the notes instead of playing them cleanly.[3]

The most common practice in African instrumental ensembles is either to use the technique of *call and response*, or build up an ostinato over which a soloist improvises; but this was not the case here. All the instruments were treated as equal partners and each player was free to improvise when he felt like it, producing a style of harmony and counterpoint peculiar to Western twentieth century practices.

Involuntary Harmony and Counterpoint

His collection and study of Hungarian folk tunes helped to influence some composing habits of Bela Bartok. He wrote sometimes in pentatonic mode and made use of tone cluster; and as we see in his *mikrokosmos* he thought of individual melodic lines without particular regard for diatonic harmonic resolutions and cadences. But perhaps it is in his string quartets that one of the important characteristics of African traditional music makes itself evident in twentieth century music with the evolution of involuntary harmony and counterpoint. Bartok's harmonies in his string quartets are many times the result of the movement of individual melodic lines resulting in what is know in conventional harmony as discord. But it is strange that whereas Bartok and others who wrote like him, were regarded as innovators, it never occured to the musicologists who came to Africa to record and analyse, for example, the all-xylophone orchestras of the Chopi musicians of Moazambique, that what they were hearing in Africa was exactly what Bartok was writing in Europe. It seems that it was acceptable to hear discordant seconds, sevenths and fourths in a Bartok or a Debussy but not in African music where these harmonies have existed for centuries and which conceivably must have influenced western composers. According to McAllester, 'any student of man must know that somewhere, someone is doing something that he calls music but nobody else would give it that name.'[4]

Polyrhythm and Pontillism

One very important characteristic of Stravinsky's music is his use of polyrhythms. He is famous as the composer who introduced the use of polymeters into orchestral music. But the fact is that polyrhythmic devices have been a feature of traditional African music for centuries and in reality Stravinsky was not telling us anything new. To European audiences brought up on a strict diet of Bach, Beethoven and Brahms, the idea of a piece of music changing pace every so often was 'new'; and the western world with its advanced technology in printing and diseminating information was able to hail Stravinsky's innovations as an addition to world music. Looking at the issue again in 1977 we must agree that the emphasis was misplaced and Stravinsky is correctly a Secondary source for this style of composition.

As with polyrhythms so with pontillism which is another innovative feature of twentieth century music. We see it used admirably in Webern's Passaccaglia and Stravinsky's Septet. But in reality is this technique not a western form of the hocket techniques used extensively in African traditional music where a melodic line is distributed to different voice parts? The difference, is that western composers have *varied their pitches* in the distribution of their melodic lines to different voice parts; whereas in African music hocket technique the same pitch is generally maintained.

Western composers have been able to very their pitches because of the development of their instrumental resources which gives them a very wide range from the grunting of a tuba to the chirping of a picolo.

Form and Process

We do know that function constrains form. Church, theatre and orchestral music up till around 1917, were written to definite specifications with the musical forms of the period in mind. We refer to the later piano sonatas of Beethoven as being innovative because he was trying to get out of the straight jacket that classical sonata form had enslaved the music of the period. But was Beethoven really trying anything new? By western musical standards, yes, but by world music standards, which should encompass African musical styles, no. He was only trying out free form, common in African music.

An outstanding feature of twentieth century aleatoric music is that it has no specific form, but rather, it is a process which goes on in the mind of the composer who develops it as the composition progresses. But again this is nothing new, since African music is, in the main, a *process* which is developed as the performers get warmed up until they feel they have had enough and stop playing. The problem was that early musicologists and anthropologists who came in contact with African traditional music were unable to reconcile what they were hearing with the classical traditions of their own music. African music was termed 'exotic' and therefore different. The Schoenbergs, Cages and Stockhausens, Dallapicollas and Boulezs were not born yet; and so the world of western music had to wait for many years for these innovators to come on the scene and 'discover' that music could be viewed as a process, rather than as a classical form. As Harwood nicely puts it, 'new musical behaviour always borrows from what has come before... the process of embedding a musical event in historical and cosmological contexts occurs throughout the world.'[5]

This is not, of course to belittle the contributions of these fine composers to world music; but music students and music lovers should be made aware of the existence of these various compositional techniques in Africa long before history books were written. In that way, African music will cease to be 'exotic' and the thought process of African musicians will be regarded as being of major significance to world music.

Orchestration

A significant difference in an orchestral work by Mozart, Mendelssohn and Stravinsky is in the manner of their concept of the orchestra. The classical concept of an orchestra is basically to use the strings as a solid foundation, bring in the woodwinds to double some of the voice parts and introduce the brass and percussion for effects. Mozart worked in this idiom. Mendelssohn as a romantic went further to explore the colouristic effects of some of the instruments he used; but Stravinsky took a different twentieth century view. He did not see his orchestra as being made up separately of strings, woodwind, brass and percussion, but chose his instruments for specific purposes and effect — and many composers after 1918 have followed this pattern thereby altering the whole concept of orchestration.

But, it is this author's view that what Stravinsky was attempting to do had been in vogue in African music long before him. The traditional African composer picks his orchestral instruments in the same way modern western composers do, bearing in mind the peculiarities of each instrument, its colouristic tendencies, the volume of sound it is capable of producing and what special effects it can contribute to the general good of the music. Thus, we find the xylophones, wooden drum, skin drum, rattle, flute, gong and horn sometimes playing together, with each instrument producing melodic or percussive rhythmic patterns peculiar to it. Following this concept, some modern African composers have been writing music with an African background blending African and Western instruments, using them as equal partners.[6]

Sprechstimme

Every discussion on Schoenberg's contribution to twentieth century music will invariably include his special use of the *singing-speaking* voice in his vocal repertoire and his attempts to notate this voice part. But anyone who takes time to listen to a ritual African music ensemble, will discover that *sprechstimme* as this phenomenon is called in German, is a very important feature of African music; but in no history book or indeed seminar or discussion on world music will you find this fact mentioned. It cannot be that western musicologists have not noticed the similarity between Schoenberg's conception and the same element in traditional African music. In a study of the music of Ibibio people of Nigeria,[7] the author found that no ritual ceremony is complete without a cantor invoking the blessing of his departed ancestors in a *singing-speaking* voice which is a very moving experience.

An intriguing question is where did Schoenberg come upon the idea? We know, for example that Bartok collected and analysed the folk tunes of his country and some of his compositions were influenced to a certain extent by this experience. We also know that German scholars like Sachs and Honborstel were among the earliest to take some interest in the recording and analysis of the music of Africa. It is just possible that Schoenberg might have heard an African vocal ensemble, became intrigued by this technique and decided to incorporate it into his music? We may never know this for sure as it was not uncommon for western scholars at the turn of the century to disregard great moments in black history in their writings. The author has been present at some performances of Schoenberg's vocal music and has found the attempts by trained western singers to perform in a singing-speaking voice rather forced, comical and contrived as opposed to traditional African performers who use this technique with natural poise and ease.

Conclusion

Hugh Tracy who has spent a lifetime collecting and analysing African music in Zimbabwe perhaps sums up the observations in this paper by stating that:

> 'Of all the arts in Africa, music is perhaps the most highly misinterpreted. When the attribute "African" is added to it, the picture they jointly evoke may, on first impact, leave the impression of a meaningless or sinister "abstract" unless we care to reverse the painting in its frame and see what is indelibly written on its back by the artists.'[8]

We sought here to 'reverse the painting in its frame' and bring to the attention of the western world what has been an unfortunate (deliberate?) omission of the primary sources for many of the musical styles of the twentieth century. It is certain that as more black musicologists emerge to write about the music of their people, there will be a need for music historians to re-write their books to accommodate the contribution of Africa to world music.

References

[1] See, Samuel Ekpe Akpabot, *Ibibio Music in Nigerian Culture* (Michigan State University Press, 1975), pp. 25-36.

[2] John Cage, *Silence* (Wesleyan University Press, 1939), p. 9.

[3] For a transciption of this musical experience, see chapter 8.

[4] D. P. McAllester, 'Some thoughts on "universals" in the world music (*Ethnomusicology*, Vol. XV/3, 1971), pp. 379-380.

[5] Dane L. Harwood, 'Universals in Music: A Perspective form cognitive psychology' (*Ethonomusicology*, Vol. XX/3, 1976), p. 529.

[6] Scores of the author's attempts at juxtasposing African musical instruments with western instruments — *Ofala Festival* (1963), *Nigeria in Conflict* (1973), can be obtained from the American Wind Symphony Orchestra of Pittsburgh which commissioned them and Oxford University Press, New York.

[7] Samuel Ekpe Akpabot, *op. cit.*, p. 65.

[8] Hugh Tracy, 'The Development of Music' (*African Music*, 111/2, 1963), p. 36.

Chapter 11
Song texts as Nigerian Oral Poetry

A poet we know possesses high powers of imagination and expression. His output can be seen as a commentary on life styles — praising, protesting and cursing human foibles and fads; reminiscing on the exploits of national heroes; invoking the might of ancestral gods; imparting knowledge; arousing emotions and making suggestions for the common good. In the western world, the poet achieves all these by setting down his thoughts in verse — sometimes rhyming with built-in speech rhythms, at other times in free style relying on emotional impact for effect rather than rhyme and rhythm.

In traditional Nigerian poetry which is oral in conception, nothing is written down. The role of the poet is mainly functional; he is both composer and performer. Unlike the western poet who can write a poem and have it performed by another person, everything the African poet has to say is tied to a special occasion; and the impact of his poem depends not only on the spoken word, but equally on his status. In considering the qualities of oral poetry, we are faced at once with the question of form, content and style. As Jaheinz Jahn correctly observes:

> '(Western) scholars continued to collect African poetry but did not investigate it as poetry looking for its stylistic rules... It has remained a treasure trove of manners and customs, a storehouse of vocabulary, a reservoir of archetypes, an inexhaustible source of the historian, a training ground for the phonecian, a quarry for the anthropologist, a paradise for myth collectors. But as literature, as poetry, it has remained unexplored territory.'[1]

This chapter sets out to ask a few questions, which, it is hoped, will help to shed some light on this unexplored territory. (a) How are these poems composed? (b) by which type of people? (c) under what circumstances? (d) in what form and style? (e) what are the performance practices? If answers can be found to these questions, then it will be possible to look at Nigerian oral poetry purely in its own right as an art form and not as an appendage for the study of other disciplines.

Different ethnic groups in Nigeria have distinctive oral traditions which are not unconnected with their particular societal behavioural patterns. The Hausas and Fulanis, for example, have a rich tradition of powerful emirates which, equated with a strong Islamic religion, influences the style and content of their oral poetry. The Yorubas and Binis have a history of stirring battles for kingdoms which has produced many war heroes and powerful Obas; and their oral poetry reflects this. The Ibibios with which we are concerned in this study, are not so much concerned with wars and kingdoms as with purity, morality and a benevolent supreme being which factors dictate the style and content of their poetry. But who are the Ibibios?

The Ibibios

Jones writes:

> 'The Ibibio traditions do not themselves provide any coherent historical persepctive, all they can offer when taken collectively is a very broad and vague sequence of events or patterns of dispersion and this only when they are considered in conjunction with geographical, cultural, social and poltical data against which statements in the legends can be checked.'[2]

The population of the Cross River State, where the Ibibios live to the south, is about 3.7 million and the main occupation of the people is fishing and farming. They are a people with a strong sense of justice and fair play. Morality among the people has traditionally always been of great concern. Very high value was placed on virginity. Thieves were regarded as outlaws liable to face the death sentence and no woman of questionable character was admitted into any of the secret societies.[3] Given this background, it is easy to see what direction the style and content of their oral poetry would take. But now we ask, how exactly do these poets set about their work? It we agree that Ibibio oral poetry is mainly functional what then are the circumstances that produce such poetry? What motivates the poets?

Style and Content

Ben Amos sees folkore as 'a communicative process'[4] and Abrahams and Foss see folk composition as being 'orientated more strongly toward the continuity of a tradition'.[5] Unlike the style of the *oriki* praise poems of the Yorubas or Hausa poets improvising praise words at an Emir's court, Ibibio oral poetry is most commonly found in song texts and invocations during ritual ceremonies. Merriam has rightly stated that 'not only are music and language interrelated in the formation of song texts, but also the language of texts tends to take special forms. Therefore, we would expect the language of texts would have special significance'.[6] Furthermore, 'folksong texts can reveal a great deal about societal attitudes, about what social behaviour is admired, hated or taken for granted'.[7]

Ibibio oral poetry actually exists on two planes. In ritual ceremonies where the poetry deals with the adoration of traditional dieties and the social control of the community, and non-ritualistic ceremonies where the poetry takes the form of social commentary on people, places and events. Ritual poetry is orientated strongly towards the continuity of a tradition therefore it has a well defined structure. The style is that of call and response with the cantor reciting his poem in song and the chorus supporting him intermittently. A typical ritualistic poem session bears some examination with regard to style and structure:

1. The cantor invokes the gods in a singing-speaking voice without any musical accompaniment.
2. At the end of this recitative, an instrument (usually the wooden drum or the gong) plays a crisp inprovised staccato-like rhythmic pattern.
3. The cantor continues his recitative, but this time, the solo instrument comes in at irregular intervals to punctuate important statements.
4. Another improvised solo instrumental interlude.
5. Cantor and chorus sing without accompaniment in two-part harmony, usually in fourths and fifths.
6. The cantor invokes the gods three times answered by the chorus without instrumental accompaniment.
7. The cantor breaks into a well known song joined by chorus and orchestra during which time he delivers his poem in praise of an ancestral god and brings his status to bear on the performance.

The procedure above is the style generally followed in all secret society sessions whether *ekpe, obon, ekpo* and *idiong* societies. A point worth noting here is that different secret societies have special musical instruments peculiar to them; and what instruments are featured during a performance and how, depends on the characteristics of the instruments. Music sound in a typical Ibibio oral poetry session, is very much a part of the structure of the totality of the performance. Two examples will perhaps make this point clear. In *ekpe* masquareade, five instruments are used in any performance:

 1 Ibid Nya Nkpe (large drum)
 2 Ibid Ekomo (small drums)
 1 Nkwong (gong)
 1 Nsak (rattle)

A bell is always tied to the waist of the masquerade but it is not strictly an instrument that features prominently in oral poetry recital connected with the *ekpe* society. In *ekong ekpo* masquerade, which is a branch of *ekpo* society where youths freely participate, five instruments, different in instrumentation from that of *ekpe*, are also used:

 1 Obodom (wooden drum)
 1 Ntakaorok (woodblock)
 1 Mkporo (large woodblock)
 1 Eka ibid (large drum)
 1 Nsak (rattle).

It is clear, therefore, that in an oral poetry recital of *ekpe* and *ekong ekpo* societies, the instruments used to punctuate the opening recitative of the cantor will be different; as will be their overall effect considering the individual characteristic of the instruments used. The dry sound of a wooden drum is a great contrast to the metallic sound of the gong or the diffused sound of the rattle. Ritual oral poetry is always performed in praise of *Ndem*, the ancestral spirits who are messengers of *Abasi*, the supreme being. Messenger sheds some light on this:

'The central theme of Annang (Ibibio) religion is the worship of an all-poweful deity (Abasi) who rules over the universe ... in the task of controlling the universe and regulating human conduct he is aided by a multitude of spirits (ndem) ... they perform specific tasks for the deity and inhabit shrines (idem).... The tasks performed by the spirits can be classified as predominantly economic, political, social or religious.... Abasi stands with the ancestors in aiding lineage.'[8]

We can deduce from this that the content of oral poetry used during ritual ceremonies, will have a strong religious flavour, coloured with references to the economic and political life of the society. The special musical instruments used during the performance of this poetry are all symbolic. Turner is right when he says that 'ritual symbolism can only flourish where there is a thriving corporate life. The symbols are related to the process of adjusting the individual to the traditional social order in which he was born.'[9]

In non-ritual poetry, the other level in which Ibibio poetry functions, the content of the poetry is designed to effect social control of the community and make them conform with the norms of the society. Here the style is more relaxed and there is more room for the poet/performer to improvise and comment on the life-style of the society. Where ritual poetry was tense and concerned with ancestral deities and their effect upon the lives of the society, non-ritualistic poetry is concerned with the morality of the community. Free from the traditional constraints of ritual poetry, the poet, functioning in a non-ritual atmosphere, is able to challenge the existing order where he finds it unsatisfactory and in many cases force change. Take the *ebre* society for an example.

The period of harvesting new yams is always a special one among ethnic groups in the Eastern States of Nigeria. Among the Ibibios, it is a time when women, generally relegated to the background in the day to day activities of a village, come out into the open to make their presence felt and seek redress for any wrongs done them by their husbands. They do this through the activities of the *ebre* society — an all-women society which celebrates its annual festival during the new yam festivities. The word *ebre* in Ibibio means yam. Since the *ebre* society is not only a moral but a protest society, most of the oral poetry used during the activities of the society extol the virtues of beauty and a clean society and challenge male chauvinism. On their way to perform at the market square, the women chant:

Idapa ikang ekikong nno
Nwong nduk enen;
Edem ete ndianake,
Edem eka ndianake,
Idapa ikang ekikong nno
Nwong nduk enen.

(Hand me my pipe
Let me smoke all the way to the market;
I am not attached to my father;
I am not attached to my mother;

> Hand me my pipe
> Let me smoke on my way to the market)[10]

This is clearly a poem of protest which seeks to establish the independence of the women in the society. Reference to smoking a pipe is symbolic; because in the Ibibio tradition, the old folks smoke a pipe usually at the end of the day when they sit back to view the day's work with contentment. Later on in the *ebre* celebrations, there is a very interesting dialogue between the leader of the group and the members which we shall refer to hereafter as cantor and chorus.

> Cantor: Ladies what is this sweet music?
> Chorus: Ebre music.
> Cantor: Ladies, you will not compromise (your views) will you?
> Chorus: No we won't.
> Cantor: Ladies you will not tolerate any nonsense will you?
> Chorus: No we won't.
> Cantor: Ladies, you serve as mattresses for men don't you?
> Chorus: Yes we do.
> Cantor: Ladies, men lie on top of you don't they?
> Chorus: Yes they do.
> Cantor: Ladies, will you continue to tolerate this?
> Chorus: No we won't.
> Cantor: Are you sure you won't?
> Chorus: No, we won't.
> Cantor: Scream your approval and let me hear.
> Chorus: Ayiriririririririri (scream).[11]

The motif of protest against male dominance is maintained in that extract; but there is also a touch of obscenity in the language of the poetry which is used very strongly and positively to make the position of the ladies very clear.

We have said that Ibibio oral poetry exists separately in ritual and non-ritualistic societies; but there are instances, when a masquerade from a ritual society takes part in a non-ritualistic ceremony as in the puberty rites of the mbopo (or mbobi) maidens. This ceremony takes place when a girl of about fifteen is sent into the fattening room in preparation for marriage. The damsel remains in the fattening room for anything up to four weeks during which time she is fed and bathed by special attendants and schooled in the duties of a housewife and mother. During here outing ceremony, when she is led naked to the market place, she is accompanied by praise singers extolling her beauty. However, during the period of her confinement, a masquerade known as *ekong mbopo* is allowed to visit her and report back to the community on how she is responding to the care in the fatteing room. If he is satisfied with her progress, he rubs her with white chalk and salies forth into the village to tell the people about her state of well being in an improvisatory oral poetry accompanying himself with a gong. If the damsel does not seem to be benefiting from her stay in the fattening room, the masquerade rubs her with charcoal and goes into the village to deride her.

The reason why a masquerade from a ritual society is introduced into this non-ritualistic ceremony is not difficult to see. If an ordinary praise singer of the village performed this role and derided the girl in the fattening room in public, this could lead to a dispute in the community with the parents or relations of the affected girl coming out in open confrontation with the poet. But in Ibibio tradition, no one ever assaults or confronts a masquerader who is free to say and do whatever he likes. So, the *ekong mbopo* masquerade is free to stand in the village square and comment, usually in a singing-speaking voice, on the virtues or vices of the girl in the fattening room making whatever comments he chooses on her lineage and antecedents without any challenge from his listeners. This is an example of narrative poetry fortified with historical references.

Another source of non-ritual oral poetry is in children's songs. Because the children who perform these songs during their recreational period are not old enough to improvise their own words, the content and structure of the song texts are fixed. The style is that of call and response; and the texts which many times narrate the exploits of legendary figures in Ibibio Folklore, usually make use of nonsense words which have onomatopoieiac effects. What we have said about the source of Ibibio poetry, is validated by Goines belief that 'African arts function... as part of religious rituals, as an expression of social organization and as recreation'.[12] We have so far examined how Ibibio oral poetry is composed; the type of people who compose them; the circumstances that necessitate these poems and the style and content of the poems. What then are the special factors to be considered in the performance of these poems? What are the aids and constraints?

Performanc Practices

We have established thus far, that the bulk of Ibibio oral poetry does not exist as separate entities as in western poetry, but in song texts either in the form of call and response by cantor and chorus or by a single performer delivering his poem in a speaking-singing voice with some form of instrumental accompaniment. We have also seen that the musical instruments used for accompaniment depend on the secret society within which the poet operates or the circumstances surrounding a particular performance. As Wisler points out, five major events take place in a ritual ceremony — impersonation of mythical being, songs, dances, definite equipment and proscribed series of manipulations.[13] So, one of the first things that a ritual poet prepares for a performance is definite equipment in the form of musical instruments associated with the society. The choice of a cantor is also very important. He must be a member of the secret society of long standing versed in the use of declamatory statements which have been handed down through the years. Together with the other members of the performing group, he must also be acquainted with the standard text of the songs used in the worship of a particular god. Cantor and Chorus must be specialist musicians with a respectable standing in the community to which they belong.

Ritual poets do not compose their own material. What they do is bring their individual expertise to bear on an established traditional format. Sometimes the cantor is permitted a little bit of improvisation during the dancing when all the prelimimaries have been completed; and cantor, chorus and instrumentalists have worked themselves into fever pitch. Here from time to time, the cantor enriches the performance by shortening a sentence here, lengthening a phrase there, introducing ululation and sometimes re-introducing the opening declamation with a slight variation bearing the stamp of his personality and his unparalled knowledge of major happenings in the community to which he belongs; and 'through the sympathetic magic invocation, he compels the divine power to unite him in ecstasy'.[14]

In non-ritual oral poetry, which is basically a commentary on the state of being of the community, the ingenuity of the poet is more evident. Here he does not need definite equipment although certain musical instruments are symbolic. Rather, he must be armed with all relevant information about the person or occasion he is commenting on and set out to express himself in a way that will be intelligible to a given society. Whereas in ritual poetry, the message of the poet can only be understood by members and associates of a secret society, in non-ritual poetry, the performer reaches a wider audience and his poetry must, for effect, be couched in such a way as to have an impact on the societal behaviour of his audience. The difference between a good non-ritual poet and a bad one, lies in the ability to communicate. Non-ritual poetry is spiced with humour, proverbs and even at times nonsense words which excite, educate and amuse an audience. They in turn signify their appreciation by urging the performer on, if they like and understand what he is saying, or disapproval by shouting him down if they find him not capable enough. At all times there is a reaction between poet and audience which regulates and validates a performance.

Side by side with definite instruments employed by ritual and some non-ritual societies, is definite rhythms which are a vital part of performing groups. The iambic rhythm is very common in Ibibio communities and differentiates their oral poetry performances from those of other ethnic groups of Nigeria. In *ebre* society, for example, three gongs of different sizes form a very important part of the poetry session with an iambic rhythmic pattern peculiar to the society. The bell (nkankika) is a symbol of the *ekpe* and *obon* masquerades; the gourd horn (uta) for *oko* society; a special kind of gong (ekere) for *ekong ekpo* society and the bull frog for *ekpiri akata* society. The idiong society is perhaps the only one in the Ibibio community that does not use a drum in its rituals. It is inconceivable to have a performance of oral poetry involving any of the above-named societies without certain musical instruments that are symbols of the society. Rhythm and symbol are all part of the Ibibio tradition of oral poetry.

Conclusions

(a) Ibibio oral poetry exists in two major categories: ritual poetry which emphasises traditional religious beliefs and non-ritual poetry which seeks to regulate the social order and sometimes provies entertainment; e.g. children's songs.
(b) Certain musical instruments are associated with some secret societies and are used in poetry, originating from these societies. Some non-ritual societies also have definite instruments associated with them.
(c) Ritual poetry has a definite form, content and style.
(d) The structure of non-ritual poetry is variable depending on the particular circumstances of each poem.
(e) Ritual poetry is designed for members of particular societies and their associates. Non-ritual poetry seeks to reach the ordinary man in the community.
(f) Most examples of Ibibio oral poetry are to be found in song texts.
(g) Certain rhythmic figurations are identifiable with some societies and used in the performance of poetry from that society.
(h) The totality of a poetry recital depends as much on the content of the poem as on the status and personality of the poet/performer.
(i) Improvisation is a common feature of Ibibio poetry.
(j) All Ibibio poetry is functional.

References

¹ Janheinz Jahn, *Neo-African Literature* (New York: Grove Press, Inc. 1968), p. 56.

² G. I. Jones, *The Trading States of the Oil Rivers* (London: O.U.P. 1963), p. 24.

³ See Samuel Ekpe Akpabot, *Ibibio Music in Nigerian Culture* (East Lancing: Michigan University Press, 1975), pp. 53-58.

⁴ D. Ben Amos, 'Toward a Definition of Folklore in Context', Journal of American Folklore, 84, (1971), p. 63.

⁵ Abraham and Foss, *Anglo-American Folksong Style*, p. 4 (Quoted by R. P. Elbourne in *Yearbook of the International Folk Music Council*, Vol. 7 (1976), p. 18.

⁶ Alan P. Merriam, *The Anthropology of Music* (Evanston: Northwestern University Press, 1964), p. 190.

⁷ Bonnie C. Wade, 'Prolegomenon to the Study of Song Texts', *Yearbook of the International Folk Music Council*, Vol. 8 (1977), p. 75.

⁸ John C. Messenger, 'Religious Acculturation Among the Annang Ibibio', *Continuity and Change in African Culture*, ed. Bascom and Herskovits (University of Chicago Press, 1959), pp. 280-381.

⁹ V. W. Turner, The Drums of Affliction (Oxford: Clarendon Press, 1968), p. 2.

¹⁰ Samuel Ekpe Akpabot, *op. cit.*, pp. 55-57.

¹¹ *Ibid.*, pp. 57-58.

¹² Leonard Giones, 'Music of African South of the Sahara' (*Music Educator's Journal*, Vol. 59, October 1972), p. 48.

¹³ Clark Wissler, *An Introduction to Social Anthropology* (New York: Henry Holt and Co, 1929), pp. 265-284.

¹⁴ Janheinz Jahn, *Neo-African Literature*, p. 158.

Chapter 12
Some Theories on African Music

Writing on the development of music in the African continent, Hugh Tracey asserted:

> 'Of all the arts in Africa, music is perhaps the most highly misinterpreted. When the attribute, "African" is added to it, the picture they jointly evoke may, on first impact, leave the impression of a meaningless or sinister "abstract", unless we care to reverse the painting in its frame and see what is indelibly written on its back by the artists.'[11]

This chapter will attempt to take a closer look at the workings of the mind of the African traditional musician, and by means of structural analysis, born of evidence from primary sources, reassess some of the theories and conclusions commonly associated with African music. For too long, sociological and anthropological considerations have tended to dominate and determine conclusions drawn on many aspects of African music; musical evidence has been made to fit with these conclusions. For example, the phallic symbol is read into the structure of some musical instruments; an innocent looking slit drum is seen as representing a naked woman, and the hammers used in playing it two men making love to her. Then there is the case of an incompetent conductor of a remote village choir giving a down-beat where an up-beat should occur; some anthropologist concludes that a down-beat in western music equals an up-beat in African music — the case of the 'sinister abstract' that Tracey was talking about.

African instrumental melody in many instances derives from, and makes use of, folk tunes; to fully understand the nature of an indigenous instrument melody, it is necessary for us to take another look at the principles of speech melody and speech rhythm. Many

African folk tunes grow out of the melody formed by the speech inflection of the words of a song. This inflection, which corresponds to the high, low and sometimes medium tones of African languages, and the stress placed on certain words in a sentence, control the intervals of the notes of a melody and dictate its rhythm. Let us again take the Yoruba proverb, *Agba ti ko yo kun, awun n'o ni* (an important person in the community without a pot belly is a stingy man); when correctly charted, the inflections in that sentence, as we saw earlier, had this curve:

Figure 1.

The question is whether the speech melody of the words of that proverb could have been translated in any other way. From my experience, I don't think so; but the Rev. A. M. Jones discussing this point writes:

'It is quite obvious, therefore, that there is a limiting factor in the extent to which a melody may leap... the magnitude of the melody leap is important. The factors which determine it remain to be discovered.'[2]

As one who speaks Yoruba fluently, I found no difficulty at all in determining the melody leap in the words of the proverb quoted in my example. I used a xylophone as a melodic guide and repeated the proverb many times, arriving each time at the same point. Next, I asked a secondary schoolboy and two illiterate workers to repeat the proverb many times and found that the workers arrived at the same magnitude, but the schoolboy's was slightly different. A comparison of all the magnitudes shows that the difference in magnitude, where it occurred, was either a tone up or down. In the final analysis I came to the conclusion that one factor — and certainly nothing else — determines the exactness of a melody leap in speech melody: that of saying the sentence with a correct inflection.

It may sound strange, but many Africans cannot speak their dialect with the correct inflection. It is, perhaps, for this reason that the Yoruba talking drum imitates only the Oyo dialect where unadulterated Yoruba is spoken. All ethnic groups in Western Nigeria speak the Yoruba dialect in one form or other, but because the people of Oyo have managed to maintain the purity of their dialect, uncontaminated by Western influences, the best examples of Yoruba speech melody and rhythm are found in the Oyo Kingdom.

Discussing African scales, Hugh Tracey writes:

> 'It is clear, therefore, that a few African communities may not recognise and employ a single scale.... A naturally pentatonic people may sing not only in pentatonic modes, but in several such modes.'[3]

I agree with Tracey; but then we are tempted to ask why they do this. In other words, when an African musician switches from one scale to another what are his intentions?

Here is an Ibo folk tune.

Figure 2.

The melody uses the heptatonic scale rather than the pentatonic; and yet we know from our studies that the standard scale in Nigerian traditional music is the pentatonic scale.[4] Generally, Nigerians use the pentatonic scale in their instrumental music and the heptatonic scale in their songs; although cases of the fusion of the two scales are evident.

The reason for a naturally pentatonic people singing in several modes is not unconnected with the principles governing speech melody. The melody leap or descent in a speech melody is not limited to points on the scale where the notes of the pentatonic scale occur; rather, they can fall anywhere depending on the inflectionary curve of the spoken word. Obviously, this means that we have more notes to play with, and as many instrumental melodies derive from vocal melodies, musical instruments like the hourglass drum or one-string fiddle, not limited by pitch or construction to the pentatonic scale, are often tempted to expand their scale by borrowing notes from the vocal idiom.

The hourglass drum (or Yoruba talking drum) from many experiments, has been found to have the stretch of an octave encompassing all the notes of the heptatonic scale. If the instrument makers had intended to construct the instrument in such a way as to reproduce only the notes of the pentatonic scale, the stretch of the drum would have been the interval of a sixth. From this, we can only conclude that long ago, the inventive mind of the indigenous musician-composer discovered that starting from a fixed pitch, all sentences in the Oyo dialect (which the drum imitates), stayed within the range of an octave during a conversation between one or more people. If two people were conversing, the second speaker took his pitch from the last word of the first speaker.

There is yet another point left unresolved in talking about speech-melody as it affects the African scale; the complete absence of semi-tones. The African musical scale is traditionally not of equal temperament; and in my experiments with volunteers speaking the different dialects of Nigeria, I could not detect a melody leap or descent of an interval of a semi-tone, augmented or diminished intervals or an internal of a seventh. Clearly then, if they do not exist in the spoken words, they will not exist in speech-melody, and consequently will not be found in the heptatonic scale.

Most xylophones in Africa are constructed in a similar pattern: the keys of the xylophones are laid across two banana stems or equivalent material, with resonators attached to some models. Sometimes the xylophone is played hung around the neck of the performer. The *kundun* xylophones which I examined in Northern Nigeria were all tuned to the pentatonic scale; but in every case, the first note was a B, producing the series: (B), C, D, E, G, A, C, etc. In a transcription of the music produced by two musicians who played on the 15-note instruments, the B was never used.[5] There must be a reason for the addition of this 'foreign' note which is one of the discrepancies that exists in the tuning of xylophones in parts of Africa. Several theories to explain this have been put forward.

Jones is of the opinion that 'xylophone makers not infrequently add an extra note or two to the bottom of the top of the series of notes.'[6] I am afraid I must disagree with this deduction, as it tends to give the impression that these notes are added without any apparent reason. Can it be that the initial note B of the *kundun* xylophone is there as a tuning guide used by the instrument maker to get his bearing right, and that once the xylophone has been constructed, the note becomes unimportant and does not occur again in the series? It is also possible that where these extra notes occur at the end of a series, they play exactly the same role: affecting a musical balance between the bottom half and the top half of the instrument.

The *ekwe omaba* xylophone from Nsukka presents a similar problem but in a different setting. Here, instead of constructing one xylophone with many notes, the instrument maker constructs three xylophones — the lead xylophone with four notes and the other two with two notes each. The three instruments together produce the pentatonic scale:

Figure 3.

But there are two notes in this transcription which need explaining: the F and the A flat, both foreign to the series. Gerhard Kubik, discussing the tuning procedure of the Kiganda xylophone of Uganda, writes:

> 'It has to be admitted, however, that there are occasional microtonal divergencies, but they do not seem to occur systematically. Considering the fact there are quite a number of physical influences on the wood in the course of the years during which the xylophone is played.... I cannot help pointing out the possibility of a chance factor.'[7]

Applying the first theory to the presence of the notes F and A flat in the *ekwe omaba* xylophone with a pentatonic series starting from C, we have to conclude that the A flat is a 'microtonal divergency' and the F is a 'chance factor'. If, as I believe, the African musician 'knows what he is doing all the time', then we have to reject suggestions of microtonal divergencies and chance factors. Is it not possible that the A flat was really meant to be A, like the other A in the series, and the flattened tone is nothing more than an 'error of judgement' on the part of the instrument maker, who has to rely purely on his sensitive ear for tuning the instrument? Having considered an A, he later on tried another A which is slightly flat at the finish. And the presence of the F?

A look at my example will reveal that the notes of the instrument are constructed by step: G-A, C-D; and so why not E-(F)-G-A? Are we wrong also to conclude that the F, like the B we came across in the tuning of the Kundun xylophone, was a tuning guide even though it occurs in the middle of the series rather than at the top and bottom? If we accept this theory, then we are immediately faced with a poser; for whereas the B was never used as part of the melody in the transcription of the music of the kundin xylophone, the F in the *ekwe omaba* xylophone was used as part of the melody. If we accept the deduction that instrumental melody many times borrows from vocal melody, are we not right in supposing this to be a case of a pentatonic instrumental melody borrowing from a heptatonic vocal style? If this is true the instrument maker was clearly aware of this 'foreign' note in the series and deliberately decided to let it stay on to enrich the melodic structure. I am rather inclined to believe this, rather than to accept the theory of a chance factor.

E. M. von Hornbostel was of the opinion that African rhythms in triple meter are iambic in conception rather than trochaic.[8] Examining this conclusion in the light of further research, we find that he was expressing a valid point rather badly, possibly due to insufficient data. In African music with a 12/8 or 4/4 time signature, the second beat is generally accented. In Nigeria, this accented second beat is a standard feature of the rhythm of small drums; it does not really matter whether the meter is triple or duple since many African rhythms have triple meters in the time of duple such as 12/8 (4/4) or 6/8 (2/4).

Jones has made us aware of the existence of a standard bell pattern throughout Africa.[9] This rhythm is conceived in triple meter; and my agreement with Hornbostel that the second beat in triple meter is usually accented (iambic), makes me lean towards transcribing the standard bell pattern in a way slightly different from Jones':

Gong

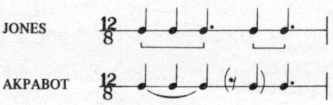

Figure 4.

Jones concludes that any other transcription is a travesty of what the African actually claps, since the African 'treats his clap-pattern as existing in its own right and not as an off-beat derivative'.[10] My experience is that in African music, there are many off-beat derivatives. The gong or hand-clap does not have a sustained tone; so that the sharp break, actually resulting in an off-beat, exists in actual performance. To ignore this is to make an incorrect transcription; for scholars have now come to accept that in African instrumental music, 'the image as it is heard and the image as it is played are often different from each other'.[11] The sharp break in the rhythm of the gong, as evidenced in its standrard rhythmic pattern, can only be discerned if we can differentiate between just how long the note should last and how long it actually lasts.

But perhaps all that I have attempted to present in this chapter can be summed up in the words of Wachsmann:

> 'Ethnomusicological institutes, of course, do not rely solely on analysis of apparatus.... There is now developing a dialogue between musicologists in the West and in Africa that promises well for the future. As a consequence of this dialogue, the inventory which was considered to be of such importance in 1956 is becoming detailed in a way that could not have been foreseen and that may indeed remove much of the danger of distortion.'[12]

References

[1] Hugh Tracey, 'The Development of Music' (*African Music*, Vol. 3, No. 2, 1963), p. 36.

[2] *Ibid.*, p. 248.

[3] Hugh Tracey, 'Towards an Assessment of African Scales' (*African Music*, Vol. 2, No. 1, 1958), p. 16.

[4] See, Samuel Akpabot, *Instrumentation in African Music* (unpublished Fellowship Thesis, Trinity College of Music, London, 1967), pp. 12–15.

[5] *Ibid.*, p. 88.

[6] A. M. Jones, 'Indonesia and Africa: The Xylophone as a Culture Indicator' (*African Music*, Vol. 2, No. 3, 1960), p. 37.

[7] Gerhard Kubik, 'The Structure of Kinganda Xylophone Music' (*African Music*, Vol. 2, No. 3, 1960), p. 8.

[8] E. M. von Hornbostel, 'African Negro Music' (*Africa*, Vol. 1, 1928), p. 52.

[9] See A. J. Jones, *Studies in African Music* (London, Oxford University Press, 1956), pp. 210–212.

[10] A. M. Jones, 1956, *op. cit.*, p. 211.

[11] Gerhard Kublik, 'The Phenomenon of Inherent Rhythms in East and Central African Instrumental Music' (*African Music*, Vol. 3, No. 1, 1962), p. 33.

[12] Klaus P. Wachsmann, 'Negritude in Music' (*Composer*, No. 19, Spring, 1966) p. 14.

Chapter 13
Nigerian Music in Societal Change

A revolution in any given society, involves change in the behavioural patterns of the people. In traditional African societies, these behavioural patterns are centred around the life cyle of birth, puberty, marriage and death. Since music plays a most significant part in rituals celebrating this life cycle, we can say that the behaviour of any given African society is, to a large extent, influenced by the musical concepts of the people. Musical concept leads to musical behaviour; and musical values are reflective of general values. In Nigeria, the advent and activities of colonialists and foreign trading companies greatly eroded indigeneous cultural values in trade, education, religion and social interaction causing a change in societal behavioural patterns.

According to Blacking, 'truly musical change should signify a change of heart as well as mind... musical change may epitomize the changing conditions and concerns of social groups'.[1] Bascom and Herskovits go on to assert that 'there is no African culture which has not been affected in some way by European contact and there is none which has entirely given way before it'.[2] In this chapter we shall look at how the concepts of traditional Nigerian music influenced religious and education change in the country.

Religious Change
The advent of colonialism in Nigeria brought in its wake a firm entrenchment of Protestant and Roman Catholic churches in urban and rural areas. To make their presence truly felt, the early missionaries condemned all forms of ancestral worship and what they

called secret societies. Since music played an important part in traditional religions, the new converts were made to burn all their musical instruments; all traditional songs in praise of gods and deities were banned as being satanaical; and organs, harmoniums and pianos were substituted as accompanying instrument to hymns, chants and the mass. Faced with strange songs and deprived of their drums, gongs and rattles which they featured in vigorous song and dance routines, the musical concepts of the people changed and with it their societal behaviour. The serene and sanctimoniously dull European approach to worship replaced their ululations and noisy drums.

Protest is a keyword in all change; and it is perhaps in this context that we should take a closer look at the role of song texts in the new religions that the Nigerian was confronted with. He was conversant with the songs of protest in his traditional culture; and here was he in Protestant churches singing hymns that were full of protest. Songs that talked of Christians going to war; of soldiers destroying the enemy; of carrying the standard banner high to tunes which matched the aggresiveness of the texts. The gregorian chants of the Roman catholic church and their dogmatic forms of worship did not allow any room for improvisation which is one of the characteristics of African traditional music; but the Lutheran hymns did. Gradually, these hymns were translated into the vernacular and Nigerian musicians started writing their own hymns based on the style of the congregational hymns and bringing in elements of improvisation in places. As more and more songs were composed in the vernacular idiom, it became obvious that using an organ or piano accompaniment was inadequate; so gradually, almost unnoticably, some light percussive instruments like the gong and rattle were introduced as accompaniment and eventually drums were introduced, however, with great caution and trepidation. But since he could not carry out all these bold changes within the established European churches, some Nigerian worshippers had no alternative than to break away and start their own church where they would be free to sing, drum and dance without any inhibition.

The formation of these new churches, with their accent on traditional self expression and musical instruments, was a source of constant worry to the established European churches as they watched many of their members leave to join the new communes. In a bid to keep their members, they were forced to make many amendments to their liturgy and introduce drums, gongs and rattles into their worship — the same instruments that had been declared satanical by the early missionaries and piled into a heap and burnt in the open.

In the new churches, the congregation was able to retain some of the musical elements of worship in European churches expressed in traditional terms. Ululation was introduced. The preacher shouted, danced round the church and invoked God as loud as he liked whilst the musicians banged on their drums fortissimo without let or hinderance. As Jahn puts it, 'in African religion, as in the religion of the spiritual, faith is expressed through the invocation of God'[3] — and invoking ancestral deities was a feature of traditional secret societies.

Dalcroze's Theory of Eurhythmics (discussed in the previous chapter) that music first enters the ear to the mind and eventually effects bodily movement causing people to react in certain ways was validated in these new religious movements that were song and dance orientated with the bible as part of a definite equipment.

Educational Expansion

Culture, as we know, embraces many aspects of human existence; but perhaps in no better way is it expressed than in music and the arts. As Bascom and Herskovits remind us, 'the degree of variation in African cultures is equalled by contrasts in the acceptance and rejection of Euro-American innovation'.[4] During the colonial era, Nigerians were made to learn songs from European countries that bore no semblance to their environment and way of life. They sang, 'London bridge is falling down'; but they had not the slightest idea where London was, let alone the bridge they were singing about. During Christmas, the story was the same. 'See amid the winter's snow' they sang; but they had never seen snow before and had no idea what it looked like. Africans had two seasons: the dry season and the rainy season; and a very cold winter which produced snow was something they could never comprehend. The situation then, was that the European teachers who controlled the classrooms, instead of allowing the pupils in their charge to develop within their own culture, were feeding them with undigested Bach, Beethoven and Brahms.

The growth of national awareness encouraged indigenous music educators to introduce African traditional music into the classrooms. They encouraged their pupils to play Nigerian musical instruments as accompaniment to their singing; and songs about winter and London bridge were replaced by traditional folk tunes which made more sense to the performers. The first tentative, and then bold, experiment with African traditional music, convinced Nigerian scholars that there was more to traditional music than melody and rhythm as they had been led to believe by the western world. It was not enough to know *how* this type of music was performed but also *why* and under what circumstances — so, they too started researching into and writing about their music from the vantage point of first hand experience. The Nigerian customs, traditions, religious beliefs and terminology that characterised the music of Africa was not strange to them; but they had to start somewhere.

Primary and secondary schools in the country established under the British educational system had very few educators who really understood the implications of traditional music; and so it was left to the universities to initiate and implement a musical policy that started at the top and worked its way down to the primary schools. For example, the first school of music that emphasized the comprehensive training of its students in African traditional music, was the University of Nigeria, Nsukka established in 1960 when Nigeria became independent. However, a few years before that, the University of Ibadan, Nigeria's first university, had blazed the trail by appointing Research Fellows in African music at its Institute of African Studies. Today, the Institute had progressed to awarding a Master's and Doctorate degree in African Studies with African Music as an area of speciality.

We have seen (in chapter 12) how early western scholars, mainly anthropologists and sociologists, who first wrote about black music in general and African music in particular, approached the subject with apprehension and condescension. The use of the word 'ethnomusicology' is a case in point. Musicological studies that deal with German, British, Japanese or American Indians are all ethnic in conception and design; but whereas we refer to studies dealing with the theory and practice of music in parts of the western world as 'musicology', we classify those of Africa as 'ethnomusicology'. The expression unfortunately has come to stay and has been used by this author throughout this book for communication purposes. But the time has come for that distinction to be erased and the study of the subject grouped under musicology since African traditional music is not a diversion from the main stream of world music, but a part and parcel of it as we tried to show in the chapter on traditional African music elements in twentieth century western music.

The result of isolating African music from the main stream of world music by western scholars in the past, was that every deduction, conclusion or theory on African music was explained away in the light of their European experiences. What they could not satisfactorily explain, they theorised about; many times coming to conclusions that could not be validated.

Unfortunately, these theories were being circulated in the form of monograms, conference papers and books into schools, colleges and libraries providing unchallenged information to students and other scholars. There was clearly a need to offer a second opinion on these writings; but unfortunately, black scholars partly thorugh a lack of funds and partly because of the administrative set up of their countries, had written little about their music, being content to accept at face value what western scholars were telling them about their traditional music and in turn rehashing them to the students under their charge.

National awareness has today created a different situation; and as more and more Nigerians have obtained higher musicology degrees in western universities writing theses and dissertations on the traditional music of the country, they are challenging some of the early writings by Europeans and writing down their own version from first hand experience. This cooperation and dialogue between musicologists of the western world and those of Africa has contributed immensely to the growth and development of traditional music in Africa in general and Nigeria in particular.

References

[1] John Blacking, 'Theory and Method in Musical Change' (*Yearbook of the International Folk Music Council*, Vol. 9), p. 3.

[2] William R. Bascom and Melville J. Herskovits, 'The Problem of Stability and Change in African Culture' (*Continuity and Change in African Cultures*, Bascom and Herskovits ed. University of Chicago Press, 1959), p. 3.

[3] Janheinz Jahn, *Neo-American Literature* (New York: Grove Press, 1966), p. 157.

[4] Herskovits and Bascom, *op. cit.*, p. 4.

Chapter 14
African Music as a Culture Indicator

Culture we know to be a way of thinking, feeling and believing in any given society resulting in a behavioural pattern which gives that society a distinctive identity. One method of finding out about the culture of a people is to examine how they conceptualize their music. For as Wissler argues, music is a stable cultural trait and therefore provides a useful basis for determining the diffusion of other cultural traits.[1] An ancient African drum in a museum may be an object d'art; but a musicologist will want to play on it to find out what kind of sound it produces and to what use it is put; an archaeologist will be interested in examining the woodwork to determine its make and age; a historian will be curious about its historical origins and dispersal pattern and a sculptor will find the carvings and decorations on the body of the instrument of particular interest. Thus an *ordinary* drum becomes a subject of intense study by scholars of many disciplines trying collectively to determine the culture of the people who use this type of drum. For according to Jairazbhoy, 'sounds which an individual selects to "hear" are also obviously related to the musical conventions of a particular genre'.[2] The background to this discussion has been excellently laid by Gourlay evaluating the role of the ethnomusicologist.[3] He is of the opinion that 'musical sounds are not things, aspects of an external world of nature... which form the subject-matter of the phsysio-chemical sciences, but products of *human* activity. Musical sounds can, of course, be studied as physical phenomenon, but that is physics, not ethnomusicology',[4] he quotes an extract from Kolinski's analysis of melodic movement of the Madagascan *Zaodahy* song: 'most conspicuous among the seven recurrent movements are two returning line up-pendulums, one comprising the upper pentachordal area G-A-E-D-C... the other the lower pentachordal area F-G-A-B-C' and goes on to ask the question 'does this account help me to understand the Zoadahy song any better than I did before'.[5] Obviously, Kolinski was not considering the thought process of the Madagascan musician or the cultural constraints that produce the musical scale he was discussing. Blacking warns that 'if we accept the view that patterns of music sound in any culture are the product of concepts and behaviours peculiar to that culture, we cannot compare them with similar patterns in another culture'.[6] The ethnomusicologist must not only concern himself with *how* an African musician conceives his musical practices by *why* he does so; and in many cases, almost completely divorce himself from the western cultural outlook to achieve his aim.

Our discussion will be viewed from the areas of music sound, song texts, legends, myths and musical instruments. For example, Tracy has told us that a few African communities may not recognise and employ a single scale which we have found to be true in the Nigerian community; but we are not told why. It is hoped that this discussion will shed some cultural light on descriptive statements like Tracy's. Most of the examples cited are taken from the author's special knowledge of Nigerian Music with occasional forays into the music of other parts of the continent.

Music Sound:

In Ghana traditional society, eligible maidens searching for husbands, go to a market place and sit down at vantage points; and as unmarried males they fancy as husbands pass by, they shake their rattles to attract attention. This information is acceptable as an evidence of descriptive research; but the question it does not answer is, why *rattles* and not woodblocks, gongs or even drums? In Ghana, as in Nigeria, young girls use beads as a mark of beauty on their waist. As they go about their daily duties, the *rattling* sound of the beads makes people take notice that they are around. Thus beads serve two purposes — as ornaments of beauty and as aural stimulus. Now the nearest equivalent to the rattling sound of beads is the gourd rattle; and so, the maidens reason that if the rattle of beads attracts male attention, a musical instrument that produces an equivalent sound will also attract the same attention. Woodblocks, drums and gongs have not got the onomatopoeic sound of many beads rubbing against one another and so they are not used. This leads us to another aspect of African culture — that of sex appeal. In western culture, sex appeal is a physical phenomenon — a low neck dress, a short skirt or a provocative posture — nothing at all musical about all these. But in the African tradition, a woman who bares herself so brazenly, would be considered to be a 'bad woman' without any moral principles. So they resort to *music sound* as their own cultural style of sex appeal; stimulating the aural senses rather than the physical ones, in their bid to attract attention. In other words, the Afican prefers what he *hears* to what he *sees* in many cases.

One way in which we can learn about the culture of society in Africa is through the various comments made by musicians during a performance. When Hornbostel said that there was no harmony in African music, at a time when the study of non-western music was known as *comparative musicology*, he was not only looking at African culture through European eyes, but had the disadvantage of not understanding the *language* of the people whose music he was analyzing. On a recording tour of the Cross River State of Nigeria, where the Ibibios live, the author heard some remarks by a group of musicians preparing for a performance which revealed certain aspects of their culture.

One of the gourd players arrived late and was told by the leader of the group that the number of musicians was complete. He insisted on joining the group and the leader chided him with the remark, 'go and play you *uta* horn with the Anang people'. On further investigation, the author was told that the Anang people were the finest *uta* players in the region and anyone who claimed to be a good *uta* player was usually asked to go and compete with them.

One subject that has engaged the attention of ethnomusicologists is the classification of scales in African music. Nketia tell us that:

> Seven-tone (heptatonic) scales are the simplest of all the scale types, and also occur in equidistant and nonequidistant forms. The latter incorporates semitones, whole tones, and intervals which are slightly less than a whole tone or slightly larger than a semi-tone, especially between the third and fourth degrees and the seventh and eight decree.[7]

The author is in the same dilema thar Gourlay found himself after reading Kolinski's analysis of the Madagascan *Zaodahy* song and wonders whether Nketia's view makes him understand African scales any better that he did before. The question we ask is, whether the African musician who performs this music conceptualizes degrees of scale construction in the same way that a European does; and when we talk of the fourth and fifth degrees, where exactly is the first degree? Is it the first note as Europeans theorise it or is it a *movable* doh? Citing an example of an amhemitonic pentatonic scale Nketia gives two examples all starting from the note C. The first examples goes, c, d, e, g, a, c, which is a clear example of a pentatonic scale with the note C as tonic. The next example has the notes c, d, f, g, a, c. Now if we here take the first note C as the tonic then that gives us another version of the scale. But, if we take the third note F as the tonic, then the scale is a perfectly natural pontatonic scale in the key of F. The contention of Bruno Nettl in 1956 that 'the most common pentatonic form is composed of ... c, d, e, g, a, with the tonic occurring on any one of the tones'[8], is still very valid as a cultural base for looking at some African scales.

If we are to get away from finding out about African scales solely from a laboratory setting, as has been the case many times, what other options are open to the ethnomusicologist? Nettl's statement that 'primitive musical instruments are ordinarily tuned in one of two ways, by imitation of another instrument or by the appeal of visual design',[9] emphasizes again the need for a thorough knowledge of the cultural setting of a society in relation to its musical practices. For example, the six strings of a harp in Central Africa are tuned to the notes e, e, d, c, a, g, producing a pentatonic scale with the tonic on the fourth note.

Trying to determine exactly what scale this is purely as music sound in a laboratory using a melograph will most certainly tell us more than we need to know; and this additional information will be totally unrelated to the reason why the African musician tunes his harp the way he does. The way the tones are chosen is a reflection of the cultural style of the people, for it is formed from the sentence *wi-li pai sa sun-ge* following the rise and fall of the inflection of the words. You don't need any additional information to reflect the principle underlying the construction of the scale used in this instrument.

Three examples from Nigeria and the Congo will perhaps explain this further. A four-tone Ibibio xylophone found by the author, was constructed for a specific purpose — to reproduce tonal patterns. It was not meant to serve the same purpose as a xylophone between each tone is regulated by the melodic leap and descent of speech patterns and a correct analysis of this instrument must be viewed from this angle. Using expressions like 'perfect fourth' or 'minor third' to describe the intervals produced by this instrument is a clear case of not delving into the thought process of the instrument maker or the cultural constraints of the people.

A six-tone wooden drum (*Lukumbi*) of the Batalele in the Kasai Province of Central Belgian Congo, is conceptualized in the same way as the four-tone Ibibio xylophone. The six tones used are a, b, d sharp, f sharp, a, b which do not conform to any recognised scale pattern because of its unequal temperament. It is used to approximate human speech where musical phrases are used to represent certain words; these may take the form of a proverb, simple sentence or paint a verbal picture; and nothing in the shape and size of the drum can be equated to any known western musical culture. To understand the *Lukumbi* drum, you must first understand the dialect of the people who play it and their cultural outlook.

Where the four-tone Ibibio xylophone and the Batalele wooden drum have no recognisable scale patterns, the thumb piano (*mbira*) and the Yoruba talking drum (*gangan*) make use of the heptatonic scale as they fulfil the musical functions. As a contrast to these musical instruments with definite tones, is the *bullroarer*, which although classified as a musical instrument, has a definite cultural function. It is used widely throughout Africa; and among the Yorubas of Nigeria, members of the *Oro* ritual cult use it for the same reason as masqueraders use their ugly shaped masks — to represent the mysterious presence of ancestral spirits. When you hear the sound of the bullroarer, you know that members of the *Oro* cult are around and everyone hurries indoors as you are not supposed to see the face of the departed spirits.

What the ritual cult members do is to exploit the traditional belief in African society that coming in contact with a spirit can be fatal; so they use the *sound* of the bullroarer to imitate the spirit world and affect a form of social control in the community. To anyone who does not understand this underlying cultural affiliation, the bullroarer is just another African musical instrument.

From our discussion so far, we can draw some clear conclusions about the general functions of any collection of African musical instruments found in a museum. For example, they are constructed to play melodic patterns and fragments in the heptatonic, tritonic, hexatonic and pentatonic scales; to imitate human speech and phrases with specially constructed tones which do not conform to any recognisable western scale pattern; to supply rhythmic accompaniment to songs and dances and to imitate sounds associated with the cultural beliefs of a given society.

Song Texts, Legends and Myths

Fourteen categories of song texts are easily recognisable in African music: (1) historical, (2) social control, (3) insult, (4) obscene, (5) praise, (6) children's, (7) funderal, (8) work, (9) war, (10) humorous, (11) communication, (12) women's, (13) philosphical, (14) ritual. All these can be grouped under three main headings: (a) praise songs, (b) songs of insult, (c) songs for entertainment. According to Merrian, 'expression of general cultural values revealed in song texts can be carried further to a study of the underlying psychological set of "ethos" of a particular culture'.[10] For example, for a very long time, the African scholar viewed poetry as a special creation of the western world and devoted all his energies to studying this art form and even writing poetry in that style. It was not until fairly recently, that those brought up on Shakespeare, Keats and Tennyson, began discovering that song texts, besides fulfilling a function, were also great poetry in the African tradition. If the narrative poems of Chaucer were a source of scholarly delight, then the historical poems of the *Ijala* musicians of Nigeria also told of great deeds by famous hunters. We have sought in a previous chapter, to show that the study of ethnomusicology also includes the study of the poetic traditions of the African.

Among the Ibibios, when a woman leads her daughter from a successful period of confinement in a fattening room, to the market place to display her charms, she sings, 'hand me a pipe and let me smoke all the way to the market place'; and from this text, we learn that women smoke a pipe and that they do so when they are in a happy mood. The pipe, therefore, is a symbol of success, happiness and contentment. Again, the text of the songs used by women of the *Ebre* society in the same location, as we saw earlier, show that the idea of women's liberation which became fashionable in the western world only fairly recently, had been in vogue in Nigeria for a very long time. They sing:

Cantor: Ladies you will not tolerate any nonsense will you?
Chorus: No, we won't.
Cantor: Ladies, men lie on top of you don't they?
Chorus: Yes, they do.
Cantor: Ladies, you will not continue to tolerate this will you?
Chorus: No we won't.

The words are vulgar, their attitude uncompromising and their posture very independent. Here the song text reveals the general attitude of the Ibibio woman which she brings to bear in her social, political and religious life.

Sometimes, a song text is interspersed with proverbs and mythical references to the valour and legendary powers of past heroes and ancestral gods. A myth, in the western definition is a story you don't believe; but it is the view of the author that legends and myths in the African cultural context are integral parts of their way of life. If we accept the definition of culture stated at the beginning of this chapter as a way of thinking, believing and feeling, and a given society *believes* in the myths and legends that regulate its daily life, then a look at the cultural traits of such a people must necessarily take into serious cognisance, their beliefs and thoughts, which may, many times run counter to the 'civilized' beliefs of people of the western world.

In the construction of Yoruba drums, only wood from *oma* and *apa* trees are used. Any other type of wood used, does not produce the correct tones needed for these instruments. Since the original drum makers had not the advantage of modern wood technology, just how did they discover this fact? For an answer, we must turn to the mythical tradition which tells us that wood from these two trees are used because they grow near the roadside and are able to hear humans passing by conversing and are this able to reproduce human tones. This is the thought process of the instrument maker, and the cultural concept under which he operates. To try to theorise on western reasons for his choice, is to impose a foreign cultural outlook on his traditional beliefs.

Again legend has it that the four drums used for the worship of the god Obatala are named after his wives — *Iya Nla, Iay Agan, Afere* and *Keke*. The tones they produce are representative of the seniority of the wives. *Iya Nla* representing the most senior wife, is the largest drum producing the biggest tone; *Keke* representing the most junior wife is the smallest with the softest tone.

In African culture, women are not usually allowed to stand to watch a ritual masquerade. But among the Ibibios, women can be initiated into the secret society because as legend has it:

> The Egbo cult was first a women's society; but in course of time men, glorying in their strength, wrested its secrets from those to whom they were first entrusted and learnt to play the rites for themselves. Gradually, the usurping male drove out the women so completely that a death penalty was proclaimed for any such who should dare to attempt to pierce its mysteries or even become unwittinmg intruders upon its rites.[12]

The women initiated into the society can watch the masqueraders in public but are still not allowed to pierce its mysteries or intrude upon its rites. The initiation concession made to them is on the strength of their being the original founders of the society. Here again we find legendary and mythical beliefs being used to regulate the social order of a community. If we remove these legendary beliefs, then the whole fabric of the society breaks down; and this is how the early Christian Missionaries were able to capture the minds of African societies, by eroding, and in many cases, completely destroying their traditional beliefs.

Sometimes, song texts incorporate proverbs which are in many cases, culture indicators. In this style of singing, the musicians use a singing-speaking voice as in the case of *Ewi* musicians of Nigeria. The performer is usually a soloist without any accompaniment; and in the course of his singing, he can chide, praise, admolish, advise, humour or philosophise. For example, the Yoruba proverb, 'an elderly man without a pot belly is a stingy man', used in one of these songs, indicates to us that in traditional Yoruba society, having a pot belly is a sign of affluence and importance in the same way as an Ibibio woman believes that being fat is a sign of good health and beauty, culturally derived from her experiences in a fattening room. All this is a distinctive contrast to western culture where the males go into rigorous exercise to avoid a protruding stomach and the females diet to remain slim and elegant.

Musical Instruments:

As a culture indicator, an African musical instrument probably presents the most diversified source of information on the artistic values, religious beliefs; family life and the general social structure of a society; for every standardized procedure in an ethnic group is an element of its culture. It has been supported that the symbol and rhythm provide the key to the African spirit and culture; and the value of musical instruments as symbols is fortified by Reimer's view that 'sound is always "felt" whether or not it is really "heard".'[13] Does this not explain the tradition in Tanzania where a drum is hung on a tree when a child is circumcized and taken down when he recovers? The sound of the drum is not heard but it is felt and conceptualized; since in many African communities, the sound of a drum heralds an important event.

When a Fulani Emir of Katsina in Nigeria is crowned, the *Tambari* drum is struck twelve times to announce the event to the community. But in Tanzania, when a chief dies, the drum, *Milango* is not struck but turned upside down. The symbolic use of a drum in Tanzania, seems to suggest to us that in moments of stress or grief, the people prefer to 'feel' the presence of a drum rather than 'hearing' it. To them, the drum which is a symbol of life, must remain silent but visible in death. To the Ibibios of Nigeria, on the other hand, a drum is symbolically connected with ritual secret societies which perform ceremonies deifying ancestral gods. But, the *Idiong* society, never uses a drum and operates as a 'clean' society which seeks to undo all the evils that other ritual societies perpetuate. A man suspected to have been punished by a ritual society, is taken to an *Idiong* priest to find out the cause of his affliction and how best he can overcome it; thus the society differentiates itself by not using an instrument connected with human suffering. The elephant tusk horn, carried by royalty in many parts of Africa, usually 'seen' but seldom 'heard', signifies a pre-eminent role in the society in the same way as an elephant is seen as a formidable beast in the jungle. A Yoruba proverb says, 'only a chief is important enough to blow an elephant tusk horn'. The family concept in Africa is nowhere better illustrated than in the use and functions of musical instruments. Bebey informs us that the Babenzele pygmies use three single-headed drums called Motopai (male), *Maitu* (female) and Mona (child) which they play on the eve of a hunting expedition.[14] The Ibibios name their four gourd horns after a mother and three male children and the Yoruba drum ensemble used for the worship of a the god of thunder, *Sango* is made up of a mother drum, a male drum, a female drum and a child drum. The most vocal and most important musical instrument in an Ibibio or Yoruba ensemble is represented by a mother figure, which is a contrast to the Babenzele pygmies where a father figure is the dominant musical instrument. What all this tells us culturally, is the importance and concern which African societies place on family life. The author in another place has stated that:

> Sometimes, a woman decides to revitalize herself by calling on Uta musicians to play for her. She kills a cow and calls a special party of friends and prominent people in her community; as the Uta orchestra plays, she believes that their music will invoke the spirit of her ancestral gods to give her back her youthful powers.[15]

From this thought process, we can see the acceptance by the Ibibio society of the supremacy of the male over female since the instruments of the *Uta* orchestra are predominantly male.

One area not much examined by ethnomusicologists, is the decorative art works on the body of musical instruments, which are obvious culture indicators. Communities with a tradition of excellence in fine arts, always reflect this, by elaborate decorations on the body of their musical instruments. For example, the Edo people of Benin are famous for their sculpture; and it is only in this part of the country that you will find flutes carved out of brass (Ikpeziken). Most Nigerian flutes are made of bamboo or wood.

Perhaps all that has been said in this chapter can be summed up in the words of Reimer:

> Trying to respond musically to sounds in an unknown style is like watching a game being played in which none of the rules or regulations or purposes are known to the person watching. One tries

one's best to make some 'sense' out of the proceedings, both in the music and the game, but unless some probabilities are discovered — some organizing factors which provide the possibility for perceiving relationships — the experience can only be 'meaningless'. No sharing can take place because perception is non-existent and reaction is therefore impossible (except the reaction of frustration).[16]

References

[1] Wissler, Clark; *The American Indian* (N.Y.: Oxford University Press, 1922), p. 155.

[2] Jairazbhoy, Nazir A.; 'The "Objective" and Subjective View of Music Transcription'. *Ethnomusicology*, XXI/2, 1977, p. 267.

[3] Gourlay, K. A.; 'Towards a Re-assessment of the Ethnomusicologist's Role in Research'. *Ethnomusicology*, XXII/1, 1978, pp. 1-35.

[4] *Ibid.*, p. 12.

[5] *Ibid.*, p. 27.

[6] Quoted in Merriam, Alan; 'Definitions of "Comparative Musicology" and "Ethnomusicology".' *Ethnomusicology*, XXI/2, 1977, pp. 193-194.

[7] Kwabena Nketia, J. H.; *The Music of Africa* (N.Y.: W. W. Norton, 1974), p. 119.

[8] Nettl, Bruno; *Music in Primitive Culture* (Harvard University Press, 1956), p. 48.

[9] *Ibid.*, p. 50.

[10] Merriam, Alan; *Anthroplogy of Music* (Northwestern Univeristy Press, 1964), p. 205.

[11] Akpabot, Samuel Ekpe; *Ibibio Music in Nigerian Culture*; State University Press, 1975), pp. 57-58.

[12] *Ibid.*, p. 26.

[13] Reimer, Bennett; *A Philosophy of Music Education* (New Jersey: Prentica-Hall, 1970), p. 96.

[14] Bebey, Francis; *African Music: A People's Art* (London: George Harrap and Coy., 1975), p. 102.

[15] Akpabot, Samuel Ekpe; *Ibibio Music*; p. 41.

[16] Reimer, Bennet; *op. cit.*, p. 101.

Chapter 15
Form in Nigerian Music

This chapter seeks to identify, classify and summarize in some detail the various forms in which Nigerian traditional music is conceived; compare them, where necessary with western music practices and see how this cultural heritage which has stood in isolatioan for so long, can be brought into the mainstream of our world educational system. Nigerian traditional music is essentially a *process*; but within that process, there is a definite structure which has, unfortunately, been overlooked by western musicologists. We have, in chapter 10, drawn attention to the fact that many twentieth century western musical forms like pontillism, sprechstimme and polyrhythms credited to composers like Webern, Schoenberg and Stravinsky, are essential parts of traditional African art forms which have been overlooked in books on music history and the classroom. But perhaps, a starting point in this study will be to find an all-embracing definition of musical form and structure.

Westrup and Harrison define the basic elements in musical form as repetition, variation and contrast; these three elements operating in the field of melody, harmony, rhythm and tone colour.[1] All these elements are present in Nigerian musical forms; but there are also other factors which influence western musical form which bear examination. We talk of the music of the middle ages, classic perid, romantic period, baroque period and twentieth century; each period having specific forms peculiar to it; and the development of these forms resting largely in the hands of composers who lived during that period. But even within this framwork, the countries of Europe were able to produce individual nationalist characteristics of any given musical form; thus we talk of Reinhard Keiser and German opera, Henry Purcell and English opera and Jean-Baptiste Lully and French opera in the second half of the Baroque period. Two factors which helped to shape the form of western music were the rise of nationalism and the improvement of musical instruments. Grout writes that 'nationalism was one of the weapons by which composers... sought to free themselves from the domination of foreign music';[2] the outcome of this was that composers in the nineteenth and twentieth century started using folk tunes in their compositions in an attempt to capture the spirit of their country. The result of this reliance on folk tumes and traditional legends, was the emergence of hybrid forms or sometimes reworked versions of already existing forms under the pervading impetus of patriotic feeling. This movement produced Chopin or Polish extraction, Smetana and Dvorak in Bohemia, Glinka and Borodin in Russia, Grieg in Norway, Sibelius in Finland and Wagner in Germany.

The development of existing musical instruments, meant the composers were able to extend their melodic and harmonic range in their compositions and experiment with tone colours; it also meant a shift in the established concept of a particular form. From about 1900 to the present, the style and form of western music has undergone an almost complete change; the elegance of a Mozartian melody has given way to serialism; the indeterminate form of random or chance music has come to stay and the individual characteristics of musical instruments has attracted the notice of composers and altered the concept of the orchestra.

Seen against the background of western music, form in Nigerian traditional music is dictated solely by traditional norms with their built-in constraints and taboos; all these manifesting themselves in the melodic patterns, harmonic structures and rhythm figurations of the music. If we add to these instrumentation and number symbolism, the structure of vocal and instrumental styles and the role of song texts, it will be possible to examine Nigerian musical forms from a satisfactoy viewpoint.

One form which is not traditional, but which has grown out of a traditional setting deserves mention here. For much of this century, the study and practice of music in Nigeria has been European-orientated; in schools and churches, no attempt was made to teach schoolchildren and worshippers any traditional melodies or rhythms. But, in the third quarter of the century, the country became independent producing western-educated indigenous composers who sought to free themselves from the domination of foreign music; so, like their western counterparts before them, they started composing music using Nigerian folk tunes and rhythms but relying on western musical forms. These new sounds were the result of acculturation; but they opened the way to the future possibilities of Nigerian music, by their exposure to western audiences and to the primary source from where the composers drew their inspiration.

These neo-classic composers who exist today side by side with traditional musicians, have been responsible for attracting master musicians from the villages into the classroom as exhibitioners and instructors. Perhaps, more importantly, they have been able to use these master musicians as informants and publish the result of their research in books and journals for educational use. The place of music in the culture of any nation cannot be over-emphasized. The ancient Greeks realized this when they made the study of music, astronomy, quadrivium; it was this tradition started in medieval times, which was replaced in the 16th century by degrees in music in English universities like Oxford and Cambridge. There is no doubt that a firm knowledge of traditional Nigerian musical forms, seen in the context of world musicology and music educational systems, will bring a fine blend between western traditions and indigenous norms, producing a more enriched world culture.

1. Ingredients of Form

(i) *Melodic Patterns*

Every melody in Nigerian music is generally controlled either by speech pattern or instrumental constraints. With very few exceptions, these melodies are usually short, repetitive and in unary, binary or ternary forms with no modulations from one key centre (or more correctly, tone centre) to another. This is partly because, unlike the western system, the notes that make up a scale from which the melody is derived, are not of equal temperament. Most Nigerian melodies will be found to be built around the pentatonic scale of five tones or the heptatonic scale of seven tones with evidence of vocal music in the tritonic scale; therefore we say that Nigerian traditional music makes use of the pentatonic or heptatonic melodies as opposed to the diatonic melodies of the western world. We can go further to state that pentatonic melodies are more frequently found in vocal music than instrumental music; and conversely, that heptatonic melodies are more commonly in use in instrumental music. Sachs sees all melodies as being of three types: logogenic (word-born); pathogenic (emotion-born) and melogenic (music-born). In the Nigerian context, the melodies are either logogneic or, more rarely, melogenic; instances of pathogenic melodies are commonly found in non-ritual music where the solo singer is allowed a measure of inprovisation; but even in that case, the pentatonic influences are so strong that the master musician invariably models his improvisations on this scale. This is where the issue of constraints comes in. For example the Hausa/Fulani *Algaita* is a woodwind instrument with five stops and invariably can only play pentatonic melodies; on the other hand, the *Ubo Aka* (thumb piano) of the Ibos, has seven tones and is capable of playing heptatonic melodies. The Hausa/Fulani *Goge* (one-string violin) is capable of eight tones and the semi-tones in between each tone; but the regional influence of the pentatonic scale is so pervasive that the soloists play only in pentatonic tones. Similarly, the Yoruba talking drum *Gangan* is capable of imitating human tones and therefore its melodic range is wider employing both the pentatonic and heptatonic scales.

(ii) *Harmonic Structure*

Harmonies in Nigerian music are usually in thirds, sixths, fourths and fifths. These are conceived in two-part form: a melody and a second part. When the harmony is in fourths or fifths, it is similar in style to the strict organum of western music of the eleventh and twelfth centurues with the second voice or instrumental part imitating the rise and fall of the melodic part strictly. The reason for this in the Nigerian context is not hard to find. Nigerian speech patters (like that of most Africans) is inflectionary in character; and if the second voice part is to maintain the meaning of the words of a song, then it must imitate the melodic leaps of the first voice part strictly. Any deviation from this pattern would result in the soloist and his accompaniment singing of two different things.

A special feature of Nigerian two-part harmony is found in the vocal music of the Yorubas who end some of their harmonies with the interval of a second which is considered discordant in western music. Two singers start out singing in fourths or fifths; but at cadential points, the second singer alters this pattern moving up to form an interval of a second with the lead singer.

Four-part harmony is not commonly associated with African music, but it exists in Nigerian instrumental music. Among the Ibibios, the *Uta* (gourd) horn ensemble of four players produces four-part harmony which spans an interval of a tenth. Because of the constraints of inflectionary speech patterns, this practice does not exist in vocal music; but since musical instruments supply accompaniment to a solo singer, they do not have to imitate the rise and fall of the vowels of a song.

Mention here must be made of incidents of involuntary counterpoint which is a feature of the harmonic structure of Nigerian music. In two-part singing, the accompanying singer may either anticipate the entry of the soloist by a few bars or improvise a fill-in for certain portions of the music where the soloist has nothing to sing. At other times, other members of the chorus may decide to hum an improvisatory portion as the soloist sings along; and since they are not acutally singing the words of a song, they are not in danger of distorting its meaning. Sometimes a second singer takes the liberty of varying the strict two-part harmonic pattern in a style that produces involuntary counterpoint, as a result of the independent movement of the two voice parts. We can see here that if there is a situation where a soloist is singing, a second voice part is accompanying him, and a third voice (or voices) humming an improvisatory accompaniment, there will be a clear case of three-part harmony and in certain places three-part counterpoint. This style of singing is most commonly found among the Ibibios, Ibos and Ijaws who inhabit the Eastern part of the country. It is rarely found elsewhere.

(iii) *Rhythmic Figurations*

Seven rhythmic patterns are easily discernible in Nigerian music — speech rhythm, melodic rhythm, percussive rhythm, polyrhythm, bell rhythm, standard rhythm and free rhythm. Since the bell rhythm is most commonly found all over Africa, and in the opinion of this writer, provides a basis for the studying of African rhythms, we shall first take a closer look at it.

(a) *Bell Rhythm*

An analysis of the bell rhythm we have shown to be made up of three Greek rhythmic modes — the iambic, the trochaic and the spondee — which combine to give it its distinctive character. In most instrumental ensembles in the country, the bell rhythm is present in one form or the other played, as its name implies, by the gong or in some cases by the woodblock or the rattle. The only possible exception is in the music of the Hausa/Fulani where either the iambic or trochaic rhythms combine with the spondee rhythm, but rarely a combination of the three rhythms; this fact is further underlined by the almost total absence of the gong as an instrument peculiar to the music of the Hausa/Fulani. A study of gong rhythms in Nigeria, will reveal that there are many variants of the standard gong rhythm; but always the unmistakable undertones of the *Konkolo* rhythm (as the bell rhythm is known among the Yorubas from its onomatopoeiac sound) is never far away.

(b) *Melodic and Percussive Rhythm*

Because of the narrow range of some melodic instruments, especially those with two tones, performers on these instruments have devised a method of turning them into rhythmic instruments; but since percussive rhythmic instruments do not generally produce more than one tone, these two-tone instruments supply melodic rhythm whilst at the same time sustaining a melodic fragment. Examples of instruments which perform this function are the *Oja* (recorder) flutes and *Gedegwu* (2 slab) pot xylophone of the Ibos; the wooden drum used throughout the Eastern States of the country; the *Garaya* (2 string) lyre of the Hausa/Fulanis; the *Amada* transverse flutes of the Tive and the twin gong. Sometimes, as in the case of *Amada* and *Oja* flutes, three or four tones can be produced; but still the accent is on melodic rhythm rather than a distinguishable melodic line. Only the Hausa/Fulani *Algaita* flute with five stops produces a pentatonic melody. There is a doubt in the mind of the writer whether the *Algaita* should be classified as a flute or an Oboe since like the later intrument, it is played with a double reed; but perhaps a compromise name would be *reed-flute* to differentiate it from the transverse or recorder flutes which are all commonly in use in the country.

Percussive rhythm which includes polyrhythms and polymetres, is a distinctive feature of Nigerian music because it provides the standard rhythms used by many instruments like the drum, rattle, gong and orchestras combining these and other instruments. The hourglass drum ensemble is an example of an orchestra that combines melodic and percussive rhythms.

(c) *Speech Rhythm*

It is possible in Nigerian Music to evolve a natural rhythm or rhythmic phrase from spoken words with the help of emphasis placed on certain words. Take the Yoruba proverb 'Agba ti ko *yo* 'kun *ahun* nioni'. When correctly spoken, the emphasis is on the italic section. Straight away we can detect the iambic rhythm the first word A-*gba* (a short syllable followed by a long one); the same is true of the words ko *yo* and a -*hun*; we can conclude, therefore, that the resultant rhythm of the sentence is in triple metre with the demarcation lines at *ti*, '*kun* and *nio*. Rewriting this sentence as it is spoken with these divisions it become: A-*gba* ti/ko *yo* kun/*ahun* n'o/ni.

On the other hand, if we take the Efik song text, '*Sob* idem *wat* inyang *keedim* ke di' we recognise the speech rhythm to be in duple metre with slight emphasis on *sob, wat, ke'dim* and *di*. Rewriting this then with the correct rhythmic division we have: sob idem/ wat inyang/ ke'dim ke/ di. This explains how accompanying musicians without any rehearsal whatsoever, are able to pick up the rhythm of a song they have never heard before — purely from the built-in speech rhythms. In an ensemble of Yoruba talking drums, the members of the group just listen carefully to the lead drummer, translate his music into words (since the intrument imitates human tones) and take their rhythmic bearings from the speech rhythm of the words.

2. Instrumentation

All orchestras or instrumental ensembles in Nigeria can be divided into two broad groups — those specially assembled for ritual worship and those for entertainment. The true form and function of a traditional orchestra can only be found in ritual ensembles where every musical instrument and song text used have remained unchanged through the ages. A festival orchestra on the other hand is hastily assembled for specific assignments — installation of a chief, a house-warming ceremony, a marriage ceremony, a birth or a death. But, if the person being made a chief or who dies is a member of a ritual society, then the ceremony takes on an added ritual significance; otherwise, the instruments used are picked at random, the music played improvisatory and the form, free and flexible.

The *Bata* ensemble used to worship *Sango*, the god of thunder, uses four drums: Iya Ilu Bata (mother drum), emele ako (male drum), emele abo (female drum) and kudi (small drum). The *Igbin* ensemble used for the worship of the god of creation, *Obatala*, also uses four drums: Iya nla (mother drum), iya agan (junior mother drum), afere (medium pitch drum) and keke (high pitch drum). The Ikpese ensemble used for the worship of the god *Ifa*, is made up of Ikpese (mother drum), aran (medium pitch drum), afere (medium pitch drum) and agogo (gong).

From these three examples, a definite pattern emerges: (i) four drums are regarded as standard in the worship of Yoruba gods; (ii) a mother-figure leads all the other drums; (iii) there is a concept of family in the organisation of these drums; (iv) there is attention to the gradation of tone colour in choosing the drums; (v) the number 4 is significant in the worship of ancestral gods who are all conceptualised as males.

As a contrast to these groups, there is the *Dundun* ensemble made up of five drums: Iya ilu (mother drum), gudugudu (two-tone drum), keri keri (low pitch drum), isaju (medium pitch drum) and kanango (high pitch drum). The *Dundun* ensemble is a festival and non-ritual orchestra and therefore does not have to conform to the four-drum pattern that we saw earlier on. But even then, the concept of a mother leading all the other drums is present. Can it be that a woman is called to lead the other drums because women talk much more than men? Whatever it is, the form of these ensembles is unmistakable and points to a well organised and carefully considered structure.

Two more festival orchestras bear some examination as regards structure and instrumentation. The *Atilogwu* ensemble of the Ibos is used to accompany the Atilogwu dance. In terms of instrumentation, it is perhaps the most varied in the country, consisting of *Alo* (large gong), *Ekwe* (small wooden drum), *Oja* (a two-tone recorder flute), *Gedegwu* (a two-note pot xylophone) which supplies the standard orchestral rhythm, *Oyo* (rattle) and *Ogene* (twin gong). The *Ida* orchestra of the Bini people matches the Atilogwu orchestra by the variety of instruments it employs: *Ida* (large tom-tom drum), *Agogo* (gong), *Ikpakanme* (horn), *Igbemaba* (rattle) and *Ikpeziken* (recorder flute made of brass). Sometimes, more than one *Ida* drum is used in the ensemble, while like all festivel orchestras is flexible in structure.

One of the most remarkable ensembles which produces a form that is, perhaps special to Nigerian music, is the *Kara* flute ensemble of the Birom people, described fully in chapter 8. Made up of four *Kara* flutes and a small drum (*Ganga*), the five musicians play what is perhaps an unadulterated example of random or *chance music*, which is one of the inovations of twentieth century western music. At a performance this writer watched in Jos, each player started when he liked and stopped when he felt he had enough; and their individual improvisations produced involuntary four-part harmony and counterpoint with some very weird sounds. The drummer played along with the group but fixed his own tempo and style of improvisation. During the performance one of the men went to urinate, while the others carried on playing; at another time, two of the players started arguing with each other whilst the others played on oblivious of their bickering. The drummer divided his time between playing his instrument and stopping to listen and laugh at his quarelling colleagues. Taken as a whole, the *Kara* flute ensemble is an example of a musical form that in conception and execution stands on its own.

The *Goge* (one-string fiddle) ensemble of the Hausa/Fulanis is usually made up of three members: *Goge, Koria* (Calabash drum) and a singer; although it is not uncommon to duplicate the drummer and singer, but seldom the Goge soloist. The *Amada* flute ensemble of the Tivs has three flutes and two drums (*Agaga* and *Ogaki*). Two other ensembles which feature three instruments of the same make are the *Ebre* women orchestra of the Ibibios which uses three gongs and the *Egwu Omaba* ensemble of the Ibos which uses three xylophones. The *Uta* ensemble of the Ibibios uses four *Uta* horns named after a mother, *Eka Uta* and three sons — *Akpan Uta, Udo Uta, Etukudo Uta* — yet another example of the family concept in naming instruments, which we saw among the Yorubas. Both *Uta* and *Ebre* orchestras are traditionally ritualistic ensembles; *Ebre* society regulates the morals of womenfolk in a community whilst *Uta* music is played for an elderly woman who wants her youthful powers restored.

3. The Forms of Vocal Music

Unlike western music where it is possible to have a clear dichotomy between vocal and instrumental music, Nigerian vocal and instrumental music are contiguous — one growing out of the other sometimes; and at other times, complementing it as we saw in our examination of speech melody, and speech rhythm. In any given situation where we have vocal and instrumental music functioning together one or the other commands more attention. For instance, in a three-man *Goge* ensemble, the main interest is in the virtuosity of the Goge player rather than the singer; but in an *Ebre* women's orchestra, the effect lies in the message of the text rather than the orchestra which serves purely as accompaniment. Because Nigerian melodies are principally logogenic, songs make more impact through their texts rather than melodies. There are songs for all activities based on the life cycle of birth, puberty, marriage, death and the worship of ancestral gods. There are songs of praise and insult; work songs and those for social control; songs which serve as historical narrative and as a means of communication; funeral dirges and humorous songs which make use of nonsense words. All the texts of these various song categories serve special functions; and since function constrains form, the form of the music is dictated by the use to which it is put. Unlike western songs which can be strophic in form sometimes, most Nigerian songs are through-composed like the *Oriki*, *Ewi* and *Ijala* songs of the Yorubas.

As regards form, there is a clear distinction between a song by a specialist musician singing alone and that by a group of people. Songs by vocal groups are usually in the call-and-response pattern. The cantor improvises his song as he goes along and the chorus answers intermitently with an unvarying chorus line which can be an exact repetition of the solo, derived in part from it, or made up of entirely new material. Songs can be used by different age groups and as birds of passage; and the form and style of Nigerian songs are a reflection of the social structure of the society; this structure can either be stratified or egalitarian. Song texts are also culture indicators from which we can test the pulse of any given section of the Nigerian society; for a complex song reflects a complex society since it is an adaptation of the trait of any given society — here defined as a group of people who have learnt to live and think together. A study of the pattern used by different ethnic groups in the country during a ritual ceremony reveals this general form: (i) *Opening declamation* with instrumental support. This section of the ceremony invokes the ancestral god in a speaking-singing voice performed by one person; the instrumental support can be one or two, usually the gong, ritual rattle or wooden drum, or as many as four, usually drums; (ii) *Incantation* without instrument accompaniment; (iii)

Song by cantor and chorus with full instrumental backing in a call-and-response pattern sometimes with some dancing; (iv) *Recapitulation* in the style of the opening declamation. The presence of a ritual rattle (used commonly throughout the country) in any orchestral ensemble is a sure indication that the orchestra is a ritual rather than a festival one.

Acculteration which has taken place in the style and form of traditional orchestras, is very evident in the composition, performance and inovations of festival orchestras; the forms of ritual orchestras, dictated as they are by traditional taboos and constrained by the uses into which they are put, have managed to maintain an unchanged format through the years. In festival orchestras, however, we now find replicas of traditional drums with a Bond street finish; a set of gongs specially manufactured to produce more than the two tones the instrument is traditionally capable of and the thumb piano built to six times its traditional size, and in some cases amplified. These innovations may offend traditional norms, but they have succeeded in bringing into popular attention some ritual instruments which the custodians of Nigerian culture had placed in cold storage for years for the exclusive use of their inner circle. The composition and staging of music dramas which base their libretto on traditional legends, myths and dieties, have resulted in a re-enaction in some of the dramatic scenes, of the music, rituals and symbols of traditional secret societies for public education. This exposure, contrary to the fears of the chief priests, has not eroded the respect and awe with which the average Nigerian regards these institutions.

A knowledge of formal structure in any branch of the performing and visual arts is a pre-requisite for the understanding of *why* traditional musicians perform the way they do rather than *how*. How they perform belongs to the realm of entertainment with its passing values; why they perform is more intellectually stimulating, encourages nationalist pride and breeds respect for the cultural heritage of the country; the *how and why* of Nigerian musical forms, must start from primary school through university. Music in twentieth century Nigeria, as in the old Grecian days, must form part of the quadrivium of knowledge in a search for a culturally balanced educational curriculum relevant to the society around which it operates.

References

[1] J. A. Westrup and F. Harrison ed., *Cotlins Music Encyclopedia* (London and Glasgow, William Collins and Sons, 1959), p. 252.

[2] Donald Jay Grout, *A History of Western Music* (New York, W. W. Norton Inc., 1957), pp. 181-203.

Selected Bibliography on Nigerian Music

Theses and Dissertations

Adegbite, Ademola Thomas.	'Oriki: A study in Yoruba musical and social perception'. Unpublished Ph.D. dissertation, Univeristy of Pittsburgh, 1978.
Akpabot, Samuel Ekpe.	'Functional Music of the Ibibio people of Nigeria'. Ph.D. dissertation, Michigan State University, 1975.
	'Instrumentation in African music: The Evidence of Nigeria'. Unpublished Fellowship thesis, Trinity College of Music, London, 1967.
Echezona, William Wilberforce Chukudinka.	'Igbo Musical Instruments in Igbo culture'. Unpublished Ph.D. dissertation, Michigan State University, 1963.
Dandatti, Abdulkadir.	'The Role of an Oral Singer in Hausa/Fulani Society: A Case Study of Mamman Shata'. Unpublished Ph.D. dissertation, Indiana University, 1975.
Ekueme, Lazarus Edward Nanyelu.	'Ibo Choral Music — Its Theory and Practice'. Unpublished Ph.D. dissertation, Yale University, 1972.
Nwabuoku, Emele.	'Benin Court Music: Proposals for future Research'. Unpublished M.A. thesis, Columbia University, 1974.
	'A field study of music as a cultural and educational system: The case of the Aniocha Ibos of Bendel State of Nigeria'. Unpublished D.Ed. dissertation, Rutgers University, 1979.
Nzewi, E. M.	'Master musicians and the music of ese, ukom and mgba ensembles in Ngwa Igbo society'. Unpublished Ph.D. dissertation, The Queen's University of Belfast, 1977.
Thieme, Darius L.	'A Descriptive Catalogue of Yoruba Musical Instruments'. Unpublished Ph.D. dissertation, Catholic University of America, 1969.

Vidal, A. O.	'Oriki: Praise Chants of the Yoruba'. Unpublished M.A. Thesis, University of California at Los Angeles, 1971.

Vocal Music

Alagoa, E. J.	'Songs as Historical Data: Examples from the Niger Delta' (*Research Review*, Vol. 1, 1968), pp. 1-16.
Euba, Akin.	'Multiple Pitch Lines in Yoruba Choral Music' (*Journal of the International Folk Music Council*, Vol. XIX, 1967), pp. 66-71.
King, Anthony.	*Yoruba Sacred Music from Ekiti* (Ibadan University Press, 1961).
Simmons, D. C.	'Ibibio Tone Riddles' (*Nigerian Field*, July, 1960), pp. 132-134.
	'Ibibio Topical Ballads' (*Man*, April, 1960), pp. 58-59.
Smith, Edna.	'The Social Functions and Meanings of Hausa Praise Singing' (*Africa*, Vol. XXVII, 1957), pp. 26-44.

Instrumental Music

Ames, D. W.	'Notes on Drums and Musical Instruments seen in the Sokoto Province' (*Journal of the Royal Anthropological Institute*, Vol. LXII), 1932.
Laoye, I. Timi of Ede.	'Yoruba Drums' (*Odu*, No. 7, March, 1959), pp. 5-14.
Okosa, A. N. C.	'Ibo Musical Instruments' (*Nigeria Magazine*, No. 75, 1962), pp. 4-14.
King, Anthony.	'Employment of the Standard Pattern in Yoruba Music' *(African Music*, Vol. 11/3, 1960), pp. 51-54.
Mackay, Mercedes and Ene, Augustine.	'The Atilogu Dance' (*African Music*, Vol. 1/4, 1957), pp. 20-22.
Nzewi, Meki.	'The Rhythm of Dance in Igbo Music' (*The Conch*, Vol. 111/2, 1971), pp. 104-108.

Miscellaneous

Egudu, Romanus N.	'Igodo and Ozo Festival Songs and Poems' (*The Conch*, Vol. 111/2, 1971), pp. 76-88.
Ong, Walter J.	'African talking drums and oral poetics' (*New Literary History*, VIII/3, Spring 1977), pp. 411-429.
Lane, M. G. M.	'The Music of Tiv' (*African Music*, 1/I, 1954), pp. 12-15.
Mackay, Mercedes.	'The Shantu Music of the Harems of Nigeria' (*African Music*, 1/2, 1955), pp. 56-57.
Phillips, Ekundayo.	*Yoruba Music* (Roodepoort, African Music Society, 1952).
Ojo, Valentine.	'Yoruba-Musik — Gentern, Heute, Morgen' (*Jazzforshung*, 9, 1977 (1978)), pp. 123-143.

SPECTRUM BESTSELLERS

	NK
Fools Rush In: Bisi Abejo	2.95
Lift to the Stars: Bisi Abejo	2.95
True Love: Bisi Abejo	2.50
Love at First Flight: Bisi Abejo	2.95
Flight 800: Dan Fulani	2.30
The Power of Corruption: Dan Fulani	2.30
No Condition is Permanent: Dan Fulani	2.30
No Telephone to Heaven: Dan Fulani	1.95
White Man in Black Skin: Adebayo	2.30
Power in Politics: Adebayo	2.95
Iska: Ekwansi	2.50
Murder at Dawn: Johnson	2.30
Black Maria: Johnson	1.95
Oil Pirates: Johnson	3.00
Without A Silver Spoon: Iroh	2.95
Our Man The President: Sowande	2.50
Survive Lagos: Cox/Anderssen	8.95

Please tick those titles required and state quantity.

Please enclose a postal order made out to Spectrum Books Limited, Sunshine House, Second Commerical Road, Oluyole Estate, P.M.B. 5612, Ibadan, Nigeria, for the amount due including 75k per book for postage and packing.

Please print clearly

NAME ....

ADDRESS ....

....

Whilst every effort is made to keep prices down and to keep popular books in print, Spectrum Books cannot guarantee that prices will be the same as those advertised here or that the books will be available.

OTHER TERTIARY BOOKS BY SPECTRUM

Title/Author	NK
Educating the Blind — Abosi	7.95
Effective Management for Executives — Nwanko	8.50
Power in Politics — Adebayo	3.95
Indexing of Newspapers — Alegbeleye (A manual for Librarians and Archivists)	2.95
Introductory University Physics Maduemezia/Awe/Ette	9.50
Development English — Banjo/Bisong	4.95
Foundation of Nigerian Traditional Music — Akpabot	5.95
Fundamentals of Management Information System — Nwanko	9.95

Please tick those titles required and state quantity.

Please enclose a postal order or bank draft made out to Spectrum Books Limited, Sunshine House, Second Commerical Road, Oluyole Estate, P.M.B. 5612, Ibadan, Nigeria, for the amount due including 75k per book for postage and packing.

Please print clearly

NAME ....

ADDRESS ....

....

Whilst every effort is made to keep prices down and to keep popular books in print, Spectrum Books cannot guarantee that prices will be the same as those advertised here or that the books will be available.